# Why You Should Read This Book

Amazon is currently offering over four million books for sale. I am confident that this one is not the best written or the most entertaining of those offerings. However, if you are like many of my readers, spending just a few hours with this book will eventually increase your net worth by hundreds of thousands, perhaps millions, of dollars. The information contained in this book is not secret. In fact, it isn't even complicated. After you read it, much of it will seem like common sense to you. However, the fact remains that you have spent twenty to thirty years in school and training for your career, and nobody has ever taught you what this book will teach you.

You are probably a lot like me. You are well educated, reasonably intelligent, and either already earning a six-figure income or soon will be. You are a medical or dental student, a resident, a dentist, a doctor, an attorney, a business owner, or other type of high-income professional. You are, or soon will be, an expert in your field. However, you often find yourself a little bit embarrassed by your lack of financial acumen. You have probably already been taken advantage of by an insurance agent, a stockbroker, a financial planner, a realtor, a banker, or a lender once or twice in your life due to your lack of financial knowledge. You may not know the difference between a Roth IRA and a 401(k). You are not really sure what you can and cannot deduct on your tax return. You know you should be saving for retirement and your children's college but have no idea what step to take next to reach that goal.

If you are like many high-income professionals, you are willing to pay someone else to handle all these things for you. However, you are worried that you are either paying too much for good advice, or worse, not getting good advice at all. Chances are that you are right to worry. Most self-styled "financial advisors" charge too much or give bad advice. Even if they are a distinct minority, there are still plenty of good advisors out there, and this book will teach you how to find them and hire them at a fair price.

If you, like me, would prefer to save the thousands of dollars per year that you will pay for good advice, this book will get you started down the path of managing your personal finances and investments on your own, and provide plenty of unbiased resources that will provide the "continuing financial education" you need to competently manage your own financial affairs with only occasional input from financial professionals.

Sometimes, high-income professionals, and doctors in particular, are a little bit embarrassed to talk about money. Getting rich was not our motivation for choosing our profession. However, physicians receive a high income for a reason and certainly should not feel a need to apologize for it. Your high income alone will not automatically lead to financial success. You must convert your high income into a high net worth in order to become financially independent, enjoy a comfortable retirement, and support both your loved ones and your favorite charitable causes. This book will teach you how to do that.

I graduated from medical school in 2003. Up until that point, I had earned less than $40,000 in my entire life. When I came out of emergency medicine residency in 2006, I had a five-figure net worth. I did not have the typical student loan burden, but I did owe four years of my time to the military, which paid me an income below the 5$^{th}$ percentile for my specialty for four years. This "time debt" was the equivalent of a few hundred thousand dollars in student loans. My spouse, a stay-at-home mother, and I saved a good chunk of our money, invested it in a reasonable manner, paid down our debts, and by 2013, when I was thirty-eight and she was thirty-five, we were pleased that we had become millionaires. There was nothing hard about what we did and absolutely no reason why you cannot do the same.

Medicine is not, nor has it ever been, the pathway to becoming ridiculously wealthy. However, despite increasing educational costs, decreasing reimbursement, and increasing compliance and liability hassles, medicine can still be a pathway to the good life. What's the good life? My definition is a life free from financial worries, a career where you make a real contribution to society, a few luxuries along the way, the ability to help others financially throughout your life, and a comfortable retirement at a time of your choosing. Does that sound good to you? Then turn the page and get started.

# Praise for The White Coat Investor

"Brilliantly simple advice for physicians. Much of my financial planning practice is helping doctors to correct mistakes that reading this book would have avoided in the first place."
**Allan S. Roth,** MBA, CPA, CFP®
Author of *How a Second Grader Beats Wall Street*

"A very practical book for physicians (and others) who want a simple, easy-to-follow guide to financial success."
**Taylor Larimore**
Co-author of *The Bogleheads Guide to Investing*

"Invaluable practical advice about careers and money! This book should be in every career counselor's office and delivered with every medical degree."
**Rick Van Ness**
Author of *Common Sense Investing*

"This book should be mandatory for anyone in the healthcare field. With its straight forward approach to tackling debt and laying out a financial plan for the future, this book saves the young doctor thousands of dollars and years of trying to figure this stuff out for themselves."
**Jeff Anzalone,** DDS
Author of *What They Don't Teach You in Dental School*

"An excellent practical personal finance guide for physicians in training and in practice from a non biased source we can actually trust."
**Greg E Wilde,** M.D

"Jim Dahle has done for physician financial illiteracy what penicillin did for neurosyphilis."
**Dennis Bethel,** MD

"A book that will permanently be on my bookshelf next to my medical texts."
**Pamela Summers,** MD

"I finally have the knowledge and confidence to say goodbye to my overpriced financial advisor. Thank you."
**Todd Bethel,** M.D.

"This book is a must read for physicians and residents. I will be giving it as a gift to my physician friends, and as a graduation present when their kids are considering the field of medicine."
**W. Devin Wolf,** CFP®

"A critical resource for the physician who wants to go it alone or for those who want a deeper understanding of knowledge in physician-specific personal finance."
**Joshua D. Nix,** MBA

"A fascinating book on financial literacy that should be required reading for both physicians and non-physicians alike. Highly recommended!"
**Michael Woo-Ming,** MD
Founder of *IncomeMD.com*

"This is the book I'd like to force-feed physicians and other "white coats.""
**Jim Ludwick,** CFP®

"A complete roadmap to personal financial success."
**Jeff Steiner** DO,
Author of *The Physician's Guide to Personal Finance*

"This book is a financial guide I'd like all of my clients to read. It provides an easy outline for financial success that nearly anyone can follow."
**Alex R. Foster**

"A great book for a physician in any stage in their career. I wish I had this book when I started medical school!"
**Joshua Smith,** MD/MBA

"The White Coat Investor provides an expert consult for your finances. I now feel confident I can be a millionaire at 40 without feeling like a jerk."
**Joe Jones,** DO

"The path to financial success and independence is pretty much the same for all people - earn a good wage, live below your means and invest wisely. However, such broad advice can be lost in the details of actual life and choices. This book does an excellent job specifically explaining how to optimize the choices faced by physicians and others who undergo similar training pipelines."
**Keith Roxo,** MS3

# The White Coat Investor

## A Doctor's Guide to Personal Finance and Investing

## James M. Dahle, MD

ISBN: 0-99-143310-6
ISBN-13: 978-0-9914331-0-0

Published in the United States of America

# Foreword

Jim Dahle has done a lot of thinking about the peculiar financial problems facing physicians, and you, lucky reader, are about to reap the bounty of both his experience and his research.

*The White Coat Investor,* though, suffers from a flaw, which is that Jim's too nice of a guy to tell you the very hardest truths about physician investors. Since I don't have his sunny bedside manner, I'll play the gruff attending so you can benefit from his wisdom to the fullest possible extent.

A substantial minority of physicians—perhaps even a majority of them—fail at investing because of a particular character flaw compounded by an intellectual failure.

First, the character flaw: overconfidence. Some specialists are more overconfident than others; no need to name names here, we all know which specialties we're talking about. But most physicians, no matter what their specialty, labor under the illusion that because they were smart enough to get into med school, that talent somehow carries over to investing. Rest assured it doesn't.

A healthy dose of self-assurance is necessary in many professions, medicine included. In investing though, overconfidence is death. If you don't know your limits, you'll have your head handed to you faster than you can say "Long Term Capital Management." The capital market system is such a complex, fast moving machine that it cannot be comprehended by the human mind. If investing makes intuitive sense to you, then you don't understand it. Think you know where the market is headed tomorrow, next month, or next year? Finance academics have been collecting and analyzing data on financial forecasting for more than eight decades, and they have concluded that no one—*no one*—has ever been able to consistently call market direction. This is a good thing to remember the next time you listen to a "market strategist" on television or on the web.

Think you know how to pick stocks? Then guess again. Every time you buy or sell, the person on the other side of the trade likely has an IQ of 160, spends 70 hours per week analyzing his industry, and has access to computing power and databases you can only dream of. And that's the best case scenario; if you're especially unlucky, you're trading with an officer of the company who knows more about it than any outsider possibly can. An appropriate metaphor for security selection is playing tennis with an invisible opponent; what you don't realize is that you're volleying with the Williams sisters.

And even the pros don't get it right. Over eight decades of scientific research show that the most successful mutual fund and pension managers top the list because of luck, not skill. When their results are followed forward, their outperformance almost always disappears. Often, that happens with a bang. The classic case of this so-called "reversion to the mean" was William Miller's Legg Mason Value Trust, which beat the S&P 500 for fifteen straight years, before giving all of that outperformance back in the five subsequent years. The message here is clear: if you don't treat investing with tank car quantities of humility, you're doomed.

Second, the intellectual failure. Understand that investing is a science just like medicine. Many financial concepts, in fact, are *more* complex than anything you're likely to encounter in renal physiology, pharmacology, or neuroanatomy. Probably the closest you might have come to the science of investing would be in a rigorous epidemiology course, where the statistical concepts are similar. You say you didn't have a lot of fun with correlation coefficients, standard deviations, chi squares, t-stats, and regression models? Then you'd better buckle up before managing your own finances; trying to invest without understanding these and similar subjects is like trying to practice medicine without having taken, and passed, classes in anatomy, pathology, and physiology. Sadly, most physicians approach investing with an almost complete lack of even the basics of finance. Jim will do you the service not only of introducing some of the essentials, but also of telling you just how important the subsequent "CFE" (similar to CME) is, and where to get it. I particularly recommend the titles he mentions by Rick Ferri, Jack Bogle, and Larry Swedroe.

As Benjamin Graham, probably the most insightful practitioner and observer of investing who ever lived, observed, the biggest enemy you're liable to face is staring out at you from the mirror. No matter how much you learn and plan, nothing prepares you for the trauma inflicted by the first bear market you encounter. If you invested through the 2007–2009 financial crisis, you know this already. If you didn't, then caution is in order. Bear markets, paradoxically, are the friend of the young investor, since they allow her to accumulate stocks at bargain basement prices; it just won't feel that way at the time. Probably the most important bit of investment knowledge you'll acquire is finding out where your "sleeping point" is; that is, the overall mix of stocks and bonds that will enable you to keep your head when blood runs in the streets. Only you can teach yourself that .

This book has taught me a lot, so I hope that Jim will forgive a small spoiler. Those who began their practices in the early 1980s were able to purchase both stocks and bonds at what in retrospect were fire-sale prices. The bad news is that today's young physicians, Jim included, won't be as fortunate. While I've just told you that it's impossible to make financial forecasts, this is true only in the short term. It's actually pretty easy to estimate the future returns of both stocks and bonds in the long run—say over the next 20–30 years. For bonds, it's very simple: their expected return is the interest rate, which, as we all know, is very low at the moment. And for stocks, it's only slightly more difficult: simply add the stock market dividend rate, currently about 2%, to the long-term average of per-share dividend growth of 5%, to give an expected return of 7%. Neither of these, unfortunately, is going to match the double-digit returns earned by investors in previous decades.

The good news, though, as Jim points out in some detail, is that you only have to replace about 15%-50% of your pre-retirement income, and that's eminently doable, even in today's overvalued markets.

Investing is a lifelong journey of learning from reading and from experience. Relax, sit back, and let Jim point the way.

William J. Bernstein, MD

# Contents

# Dedication

To Katie, Whitney, Maren, and Jonas,
Who help me to remember what matters most in life

# Acknowledgements

In many ways, this book was a group project and could never have been completed without the assistance of others. I am particularly grateful to William J. Bernstein not only for writing the foreword, but for the inspiration provided by his example and writings. I was a "BernsteinHead" before I was ever a "Boglehead." Mike Piper, CPA, also deserves special recognition for literally teaching me the class on writing and self-publishing a book. Rick Ferri sat next to me in that class, but more importantly, has been instrumental in shaping my investing and my writing. I would like to thank Ashley Chandler for the cover design, Joel Remke for the photos, and Doug Russell for grammatical editing.

I am also grateful for the following individuals who either reviewed the manuscript or shared personal experiences that improved the book: Joshua D. Nix, MBA, Joseph T. Buco, CHBC, Joshua Smith, MD, Greg E. Wilde, MD, Jim Ludwick, CFP®, Paul DiDomenico, MD, Jeffrey V. Anzalone, DDS, Pamela Summers, MD, Keith Roxo, MS3, Niraj H. Pahlajani, MD, Eugene A. Lechmanik, MD, Allan S. Roth, H. Nelson Conley, MD, Taylor Larimore, Hamilton Lempert, MD, Alex R. Foster, Dennis Bethel, MD, W. Devin Wolf, CFP®, Ravi K. Desai, MD, Jeff Steiner, DO, Josh Mettle, Douglas Segan, MD, JD, and Joseph L. Luehrmann, Jr.

# Chapter One
# The Big Squeeze

*"Everybody who's a physician, who makes vaccines, who wants to find the cure for cancer. Everybody who wants to do any medical good for humankind got the passion for that before he or she was 10."* — Bill Nye

It will seem odd to a nonphysician to see this book. "How can a career in medicine NOT lead to the good life?" you may wonder. The idea that you should become "a doctor or a lawyer" to get rich because "doctors and lawyers are rich" is well entrenched in our cultural lore. Unfortunately, this "truism" is becoming less and less true every year. In fact, for the attorneys, the phrase is already essentially false. Sometime in the last decade or two, law schools seem to have transitioned into for-profit institutions, increased their class sizes to increase their profits, and pumped out thousands of law school graduates, apparently far in excess of the actual need for attorneys. The National Association for Law Placement (NALP) Survey of the class of 2011 law school graduates found that only 85.6% of law school graduates found employment after graduation, and only 65.4% obtained a job that actually required bar passage. Of those in a job where bar passage was required, the median salary was only $61,500.

Medicine has fared far better than Law in the last few years, mostly because unlike attorneys, the demand for fully trained physicians continues to rise. Physicians are facing their own challenges, however, which I like to refer to as "The Big Squeeze," which is simply this: it costs more to get the job, the job pays less once you get it, and increasing liability and compliance concerns make the job less pleasant.

### The Tuition Bubble

Many pundits have referred to the rapidly increasing cost of higher education as "a bubble," akin to the technology stock bubble of the late 1990s, which burst in 2000–2002 or the real estate bubble whose bursting caused "The Great Recession of 2008." I have no idea if we are in a tuition "bubble" or not, since the term "bubble" implies it will burst at some point, and the trend doesn't seem to be slowing, much less reversing, anytime soon. When I started medical school at the University of Utah in 1999, in-state tuition was about $10,000 per year (it had been $8,000 just a year or two before). In 2013–2014, in-state tuition will be $32,000 per year. The price has essentially quadrupled in just sixteen years. If tuition were increasing at the general rate of inflation, it would be $11,600 in 2013, not $32,000. Is the education really four times better than it used to be? I highly doubt it. In fact, it has apparently gotten so bad that a few years ago they had to institute mandatory classroom attendance since so few students were attending, preferring to learn from texts, online resources, the class syllabus, and note-taking services. Is the job the degree qualifies you for paying you four times as much? Certainly not.

### Student Loan Interest Rates

When my class graduated from medical school in 2003, those of us with student loans refinanced them at ridiculously low rates. Many of my classmates ended up with a fixed rate under 1%. Beginning in 2006, Stafford loans for graduate students were fixed at 6.8% and stayed that way until 2013, despite the fact that overall interest rates had dramatically decreased thanks to the actions of the Federal Reserve in response to The Great Recession of 2008. I found it absolutely bizarre that in 2013 I could get a 15-year fixed loan on a mortgage for less than 3%, but a medical student couldn't get a student loan paid back over ten years for less than 6.8%.

The student loan may be unsecured like a credit card debt (as opposed to a mortgage that is secured by the property it is taken out on), but it also cannot be discharged in bankruptcy except in very limited circumstances. To make matters worse, a medical student can only take out up to $40,500 in Stafford loans each year, which doesn't go very far when tuition alone often exceeds that figure. In the 2013-2014 school year, according to the Association of American Medical Colleges, tuition and fees averaged $31,783 for residents at public medical schools, $55,294 for non-residents at public schools, and $50,476 at private schools. DO schools are not much better, with tuition and fees averaging $41-45,000 per year according to the American Association of Colleges of Osteopathic Medicine. (AACOM) Some students are paying over $80,000 per year in tuition and fees alone. These high costs force a student, or his parents, to borrow additional money through the Direct Plus Loan Program, where the interest rate is even higher.

## Worsening Loan Terms

A larger amount of money borrowed at a higher interest rate is bad enough. Unfortunately, like a late-night commercial for a $19.99 knife set, all I can say is "But wait, there's more!" The loans are not just at a higher interest rate. Starting in 2012, they are unsubsidized. The government will no longer pay the interest on Stafford loans while you are in school. Hardship deferrals are also difficult for residents to qualify for. That means that from the moment you take out a Stafford loan, the interest starts accruing at five, six, or even eight percent per year. It is easy to see using a financial calculator or a spreadsheet's "Future Value" function that if you don't make any significant payments in residency on a $40,500, 6.8% loan taken out as a first year medical student (MS1), you will actually owe $73,214 upon completion of a 5-year residency. If you borrowed another $20,000 as a Direct Plus Loan as an MS1, the loan burden just from your first year of medical school would be $112,863! If you were attending a more expensive medical school, such as Tufts University, where the 2013– 2014 tuition is $56,080 and the total cost of attendance is over $80,000 per year, your loan burden from four years of medical school at the end of a 5-year residency could be as much as $555,000! It doesn't take a math genius to see that current MS1s at expensive medical schools are likely to finish residency owing something in the neighborhood of $600,000 at a high interest rate. At a blended interest rate of 6%, it will cost a physician $36,000 a year just to service the interest on those loans. These figures assume, of course, that the student has no student loans from his undergraduate years. Loans from an expensive undergraduate institution combined with an expensive medical school are a recipe for financial disaster!

The Association of American Medical Colleges (AAMC) surveys medical school graduates every year about the amount of debt they have. On the survey of 2013 graduates, indebted students owed an average of $204,995 in educational debt. This is a 31% increase from the $155,982 reported by 2007 graduates. After 3–7 years of additional high interest compounding during residency, the figures will be much worse. Figure 1 demonstrates the trend.

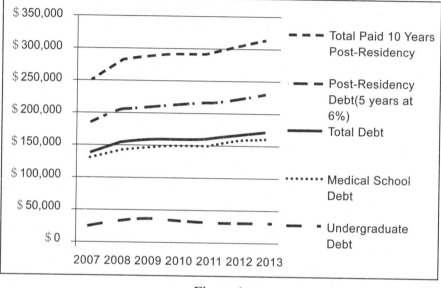

**Figure 1**

Figure 1 does not count any credit card debt, car loans, or mortgage debt. Using these averages also hides the fact that a few students have incredible student debt burdens. In 2013, 29.3% owed more than $200,000 in educational debt. That figure was just 15.9% in 2007. A debt of $300,000 compounded at 6% over a 5-year residency will grow to over $400,000 at residency completion and over $545,000 by the time the debt is paid off!

In 2013, Congress changed the formula for how student loan rates will be calculated. The formula is now the 10-year treasury rate plus 3.6% for graduate Stafford loans and the 10-year treasury rate plus 4.6% for PLUS loans. The good news is that this lowered rates for 2013–2014 to 5.41% and 6.41% respectively.

The bad news is that if interest rates rise significantly from their historic lows, student loan rates could be even higher in the future than they are now.

Long-term borrowers, such as mortgage holders, are always on the lookout for opportunities to lower their interest rate by refinancing and consolidating their loans. This option, unfortunately, wasn't available to a student borrower from 2006 to 2013. Since student loan interest rates don't fluctuate with changes in general interest rates, there really weren't opportunities to refinance student loans. The government did allow loan consolidation, but the consolidation process essentially took your average interest rate and then rounded it UP to the nearest 1/8%. Thankfully, beginning in late 2013, some options for student loan refinancing have finally appeared on the market, allowing physicians to refinance their medical school debt into the 5% to 6% range. Bear in mind when refinancing that refinanced loans are not forgiven at death like the original government student loans nor are they dischargeable in bankruptcy.

## Decreasing Physician Pay

Clearly, it will cost a great deal more to become a physician in the future. This factor alone could be easily dealt with if physician pay were increasing at a similar rate. Unfortunately, physician pay is not increasing. In fact, it is decreasing. The Center For Studying Health System Change did a study from 1995 to 2003. They found that while most professional and technical salaries increased 7%, physician salaries decreased by 7% in inflation-adjusted terms. In a paper published in JAMA in November 2012, Seabury et al. compared median physician earnings from 1996 to 2000 with median physician earnings from 2006 to 2010 and found a decrease from $166,733 to $157,751. This only looked at physicians over thirty-five (since many doctors under this age are in training) and was NOT adjusted for inflation. If you adjust for inflation, that represents a decrease in real earnings of over 28%. Clearly, physicians are earning less than they used to and significantly less when you adjust for inflation.

Part of this decrease in salary is explained by the trend of physicians leaving self-employment for employee positions. In recent years, the number of self-employed physicians has decreased from about two-thirds to one-third of doctors. An employee, by definition, is never paid what that person is worth. A business owner who expects to make a profit cannot pay an employee exactly the amount of money the employee brings into the business or there is no profit left for the business owner.

### Increasing Liability and Regulatory Costs and Hassles

Many physicians cite increasing medical liability insurance premiums as contributing factors to their decreasing take-home salaries and decreasing work satisfaction. The data, however, shows that insurance premiums have actually been quite stable over the last five to six years. A much more significant expense and hassle for most physicians is the increasing regulation of the last few years, including the Emergency Medical Treatment and Labor Act (EMTALA), the Health Insurance Privacy and Portability Act (HIPPA), mandatory electronic medical records (EMR), and the Patient Protection and Affordable Care Act. Such measures are certainly contributing to the trend of physicians moving from solo practice and small groups into larger groups and hospital employment situations. It is nearly impossible for a typical solo practice to keep up with the new regulations much less pay the cost of complying with them.

### The Big Squeeze

It costs more each year to become a physician, yet physicians are not only paid less each year but are also faced with more regulatory and legal burdens. None of this comes as news to an attending-level physician but should explain to the nonphysician reader (as well as some of the more idealistic premedical and medical students) why a book like this is even necessary. The fact is that medicine, like law, is no longer a guaranteed pathway to riches. In fact, thousands of physicians around the country literally live hand to mouth. But it doesn't have to be this way. By making solid financial decisions, doctors can still practice the profession they love AND achieve financial independence and freedom. In short, medicine can still be a path to "the good life," and I am going to show you how beginning in the next chapter.

**Summary of Chapter 1**

- Medical school is becoming more expensive.
- The after-inflation income of physicians is decreasing.
- Increasing bureaucracy and liability are making the practice of medicine more onerous.
- Physicians can still have a great life by optimizing their personal finance and investing practices

# Chapter Two
# Millionaire by 40

*"If it weren't for baseball, many kids wouldn't know what a millionaire looked like."* — Phyllis Diller

At some point along the way during my training, I thought it would be cool to be able to say I was a millionaire by age forty. I even ran the numbers to see if it could be possible. My projections at that point suggested that I probably wouldn't make it. I would likely be forty-one or forty-two by the time our net worth reached $1 million. Actually, though, we ended up making a little more money than expected, saving a little more money than expected, and doing better on our investments than expected thanks to the strength of the bull market coming out of The Global Financial Crisis of 2008. Instead of a "millionaire by forty" I was a "millionaire at thirty-eight."

### Millionaire At 38

I realized I had become a millionaire on November 16, 2013. It had probably happened a few days before, when my monthly paycheck hit the bank account. It took my wife and me just a little over ten years from medical school graduation to become millionaires. She worked for just one of those years, and for six of those years, we had a taxable income under $100,000.

### Calculating Net Worth

When you have financial goals, it is important to track progress toward them. An annual net worth calculation is an easy way to see how you are doing. We have done this each year since I started earning a salary. There are an infinite number of formulas for how to calculate it, but basically you subtract your liabilities (such as student loans, car loans, credit card loans, and mortgages) from your assets (such as bank accounts, investments, and property values), and the difference is your net worth. I try not to make it too complicated. I don't count such consumer goods as furniture, clothing, and cars as assets because they are all depreciating anyway. I count our bank accounts, retirement accounts, investments, the value of my small business (The White Coat Investor, LLC), and the equity in our rental property and primary residence. Our only debt is the mortgages on those two properties. Taken all together, Figure 2 shows what our net worth has looked like since I got out of medical school.

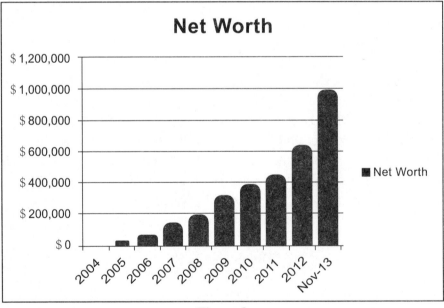

**Figure 2**

The casual reader may not be familiar with typical physician salaries. Having a net worth of a million dollars isn't that impressive for a couple that makes $1 million a year. The easiest way for me to demonstrate our income over the last ten years is to use my "Medicare Income" as recorded by the IRS. You don't want to use Social Security income, since it is capped at a certain amount ($117,000 for 2014), which is below the typical physician income. Medicare income includes every dollar you earn, including money put into retirement accounts. It does miss a few things, for example, investment income and tax-free income, such as the housing and subsistence allowances I received in the military. It also doesn't include my wife's income from the single year she worked as a teacher.

However, Medicare Income is an easy number to obtain, and it will give you some idea of how the last decade has looked for us regarding income. Keep in mind that I was in residency from 2003 to 2006, served in the military until 2010, and then was an employee until I became a partner midway through 2012. Figure 3 demonstrates our income over the decade since medical school graduation.

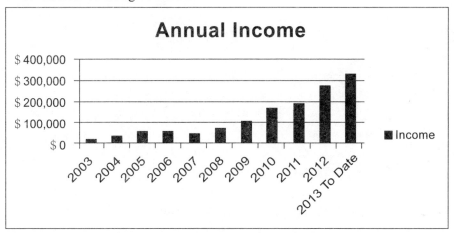

**Figure 3**

**Get Rich Slowly**

I post these figures not to brag, since there are plenty of doctors out there who have a higher income and a higher net worth than I do, but to point out that becoming a millionaire by age forty is very doable for many physicians. We received no inheritance, bought no winning lottery ticket, and never had a ridiculously high income. If becoming a millionaire is "getting rich," then we did so the old-fashioned way—by working hard, saving a good chunk of income, and investing it in a reasonable manner. To me, the most impressive thing is not that I had earned a total of ~$1.36 million in the last ten years (an average of $136,000 a year), but that I still had $1 million of it, or 73% of everything I had earned since graduation.

We didn't do this by maintaining a ridiculously high savings rate. The lion's share of our net worth certainly came from brute savings, but a significant chunk came from paying off debt and smaller amounts from appreciation of our properties and investments. Each year I also calculate our "savings rate" (essentially money put into savings divided by our total income), and that figure has fluctuated from as little as 5% to as much as 46% but has averaged right around 30%. As a percentage of our net worth, 56% came from brute savings, 19% from paying down loans, 6% from appreciation of properties, 2% from the value of my website, and only 17% from actual investment returns.

### I'm Not the Only One

One thing I enjoy most about blogging on The White Coat Investor website (http://whitecoatinvestor.com) is hearing the financial success stories of other physicians. I'd like to share a few such stories with you in the hope that they will inspire you as well.

### An Ophthalmologist's Story

I started investing in the stock market when I was ten years old and learned from experience that index fund investing is far better than stock picking. I learned to be frugal in college, at one point being able to boast that I ate on less than $1 per day. The frugality continued into medical school, residency, and to some extent even today. Early in life, I heard my uncle say, "If you are willing to live like no one else will early in life, then you can live like no one else can later in life." I maxed out a personal and spousal Roth IRA during residency.

I believe in the principle that saving money is easier than earning money (a dollar saved is worth a dollar, while a dollar earned is only worth about fifty cents due to taxes). When I started out in private practice as an ophthalmologist four years ago, our practice overhead was 68% my first year. Over the next two years, I helped our ten physician group cut our overhead from 68% to 52%, which essentially gave each of us a 50% raise without anyone needing to work a bit harder. Also, when I joined the group, we rented our five offices. It has taken four years, but we now own four of our five offices, an investment providing returns of around 15%.

I am thirty-eight, and we are a one-income family. We save 40% of our gross income, roughly 30% goes to taxes, we donate 12%, and we live off of the remaining 18%. It is no coincidence that what we spend was listed last, as the savings and donations are the first to come out of our paycheck. I drive a 13-year-old Honda Accord that I bought used. My wife drives a 6-year-old Sienna minivan, also purchased used. Some may say it is easy to save when you have a high income, but the savings and donations percentages I listed have essentially remained the same regardless of whether we were making $45,000/yr as a resident or the much higher income that we now earn. If you are not disciplined enough to save on a $45,000 income, it won't be any easier on a six-figure income. I am four years out of fellowship and have a net worth of $1.8 million.

All of our debts are paid off other than our 15-yr mortgage and commercial real estate loans on our office buildings. We plan to be in a position to be able to retire by age fifty, though I will probably just cut back at that time. We have four kids, live in a nice house, go on one or two nice vacations per year and don't feel like we really have any unmet wants. We get a lot of joy in helping others, especially those in need, with our time, money, and professional resources (pro bono work, humanitarian trips). The main reason we feel financially secure is not because of our income but rather because of the many years of sacrifice that were required to get our financial house in order FIRST. Financial security is much more comforting and lasts much longer than that new Audi A6 that zips past me on the freeway.

### An Emergency Doc's Story

I finished residency at age thirty in emergency medicine in 1996 having gone straight through with my education. I had $140,000 in educational debt. I considered it a mortgage taken out on my brain, and I hoped nobody would foreclose. During residency, I got married, and we lived a fairly reasonable life financially. We were renting an apartment until the last year of my residency when I signed a contract to work in the same city I was graduating in, and we decided to buy a house. I had to work an extra three moonlighting shifts a month in order to make the mortgage until graduation. We worked very hard to keep our lifestyle and our expenses not much more than what we were spending during residency.

After three years of maintaining our expenses and putting every extra dollar toward the educational debt, it was gone. We then had two children, and our cars needed replacing, so our expenses went up a little bit. However, I made saving for retirement a priority and started 529 plans for the kids as they were born. We decided to have my wife stay home and raise our children instead of working. Unfortunately, the stock market wasn't very cooperative. I started investing in 1999 right before the dot-com crash of 2000–2002 and then again in 2008. Through it all, I continued to save. In 2006, I hit the $1 million mark, and now in 2013 I'm just under $2.5 million. We take vacations every year, but I still drive a 15-year-old Subaru, and my wife drives a minivan. We do not live extravagantly, but we do not live as paupers. Every bonus went into savings, and we never tried to keep up with the Joneses.

### The Story of Two Military Family Docs

I married another Army family practice resident and shortly afterward calculated how much we'd need to save to retire at fifty-five. We came up with an amount that was about 25% of our income back then and usually exceeded that amount each year. I guess we probably felt the military pay raises and new bonuses were surplus rather than already spent. When we had a child, we added on a monthly amount for paying for college, and we started banking one of our entire incomes to be sure we could live off a single income when we got a chance to have a stay-at-home parent.

We put our money into Vanguard funds regularly, and I enjoyed reporting to my husband (and brother, an actuary) how close we were to our goal and eventually how far ahead of it we were. We seemed to live more frugally, older cars and less fancy homes or private school, than our one-income family physician colleagues, but we have always valued freedom over spending. I'm fifty, and he's forty-eight, and we're each a millionaire, not even including his Army pension. We have both retired from medicine, although I nag him to maintain his credentials in case something happens. I am running for state office and only consider this retirement a sabbatical (I'll have time to do locums if elected). We live pretty well, much better than we would be if we were chained to our jobs. Obviously, we decided medicine wasn't worth the hassle anymore given our other options.

### An Oral and Maxillofacial Surgeon's Story

I just did the basics—getting rid of debt or refinancing it as soon as possible. I still have some debt but nothing over 4%. I married a dentist who happened to be a great saver early in residency and graduated without any consumer debt. She was able to work part-time, and we had two children in residency. We hadn't saved much, but at least we didn't create any new debt. I bought my own practice right out of residency, but I didn't buy a Mercedes, just an old Toyota. We believe everything is negotiable, and I worked hard to build up my practice quickly. Now instead of pharmaceutical representatives bringing in lunch to the staff, I have banks bringing it in trying to get my business. After building up the practice and limiting overhead, I now have a million dollar salary.

We bought a fixer-upper house and fixed it up without borrowing. We live off 25% of my gross, the government takes 38%, and we stash the rest (37%) into relatively conservative investments. I use a financial planner but negotiate fees carefully and feel that thus far he is earning them.

A recent experience helped me feel like a successful parent and saver. My 6-year-old daughter, after spending some time riding in the Range Rover her neighborhood friend's family drives, asked me why we were so poor. Apparently, she thought that because we drive a Toyota and don't eat out as much as her friend (whose family has some serious debt issues and is running as fast as they can on the hedonic treadmill) that we were poor!

### A Family Physician's Story

I am currently 59 years old and retired seven years ago at age 52. I graduated from medical school in 1977, graduated from residency in 1980; and was in general practice continuously until my retirement in 2007. I was 45 in 1999 when our net worth passed the $1 Million mark. In looking back, there are a number of important factors that allowed me to retire early, even as a family doctor.

First, living below your means is critical. My wife and I have always lived modestly and did not adhere to the "rich doctor" lifestyle. I was never interested in a large "doctor mansion"; fancy car; expensive hobbies; or frequent trips. We didn't live like paupers, understand me, but our outgoing expenses were not at the level of our peers.

Second, debt aversion. I paid myself a salary through my Corporation; and then received a variable bonus at the end of each year. This bonus ranged from $3,000-$30,000. In every instance, I applied this bonus towards paying off my mortgage early. I did not increase my lifestyle as a result of the bonus. I converted a 15 year, 13% fixed mortgage to a nine year, 7% mortgage by refinancing twice and saved $85,000 in interest payments.

Third, my wife and I had similar thoughts about money management, and were prodigious savers. We saved at least 20% of our combined salaries during our working years and regularly contributed to our investments. We always maximized our 401(k) contributions, and even managed to save a half million dollars in taxable accounts.

Fourth, the more that I learned financially, mostly following principles espoused by Jack Bogle, the better we seemed to do. Fifth, we never carried a balance on a credit card. Sixth, I had purchased a whole life policy early on in my career, and surrendering that freed up significant money I could invest in more profitable ways.

### The Good Life

As the stories above demonstrate, life is about much more than just accumulating money. Money might not bring happiness, but having been both rich and poor, I definitely prefer rich. Purists might argue that a mere million dollars doesn't actually qualify you as rich, since it can really only support an income of about $40,000 a year. Our financial goal isn't to die with a million bucks in the bank or millions in investments.

My family's goal is to live the good life, and as near as I can tell, we've achieved it. We live a comfortable life. We never fight about money. We don't have to check the bank account prior to making a purchase of less than five figures. We never have to tell our children they can't participate in an activity because we can't afford it. Our vacations are limited more by our available time than money. We have all the "stuff" we need, including a large house with a 100-mile view, two SUVs, and a garage full of toys. We have good health, disability, property, life, and liability insurance to protect us from financial catastrophes. My wife can spend her time with our children, working out, and volunteering in the community. I work 120 hours a month at my dream job, run an increasingly successful side business and have time to enjoy numerous hobbies. We've also donated over six figures to charity in the last decade. In short, we're living the good life. With good financial decision making, you can too.

**Summary of Chapter 2**

- You can become a millionaire by forty as a physician.
- The key to doing this is to rapidly convert your income into wealth.
- Money isn't the most important thing in life, but mismanaging it can sure make you miserable.

**Recommended Additional Reading**

http://whitecoatinvestor.com/stupid-doctor-tricks-biggest-financial-mistakes/

# Chapter Three
# If I Had a Million Dollars

*"If I had a million dollars, we wouldn't have to eat Kraft dinner. But we would eat Kraft dinner, of course, we would. We'd just eat more."*
— The Barenaked Ladies

The phrase "millionaire" was originally coined in France in the 1700s but really only came into usage in the English-speaking world in the 1800s. A millionaire today certainly isn't what it used to be, not only due to increasing prosperity but primarily due to inflation, as can be seen in Table 1. In fact, there are now nine million households (8% of the population) in the United States with a net worth of $1 million or more, not including their primary residence. That's not exactly an exclusive club. In fact, to be the equivalent of a millionaire in 1914, you'd need $23 million today. It would be a very unusual physician who ever reached that mark. Most currently practicing physicians probably won't ever be the equivalent of a "1950 millionaire." Doctors just don't make that much money.

### The 4% Rule

Financial planners often use a rule called the 4% rule to determine how much of your nest egg you can spend each year in retirement. The Trinity

Study famously demonstrated that you can spend about 4% of your retirement portfolio each year, adjusted up for inflation, and expect to have the money last throughout your retirement.

| Millionaire in | Inflation-Adjusted Net Worth Equivalent in 2013 |
|---|---|
| 1914 | $23,028,000.00 |
| 1950 | $9,799,100.00 |
| 1975 | $4,420,000.00 |
| 1990 | $1,807,500.00 |
| 2000 | $1,364,200.00 |

**Table 1**

In this study, the authors took various asset allocations, from 100% stocks to 100% bonds. They then took the historical returns for these portfolios and applied various withdrawal rates over periods of time from fifteen to thirty years to determine in what percentage of the historical time periods the portfolio would not have run out of money during that time period. See Table 2 for their results. For example, a 5% withdrawal rate (increased with inflation each year) applied to a 75% stock portfolio over a period of twenty-five years would have lasted the entire twenty-five years in 87% of historical periods studied.

Some purists might argue that the "safe withdrawal rate" is 3% or 3.5%, and that's all well and good. The point of the study was that you CANNOT spend the 10%, 8%, or even 6% that many financial advisors had been recommending at the time and expect your money to last. The 4% rule is also a great rule of thumb that allows you to convert between income and wealth. A $1 million portfolio can provide an income of $40,000 a year before tax. By that standard, a million dollars doesn't seem like all that much. Most physicians retiring now are probably going to want more income than that and thus will need a larger retirement portfolio. As I discuss in chapter 7, however, they won't need to replace the 80%–100% of preretirement income that many advisors mistakenly recommend.

| Retirement Portfolio Success Rates by Withdrawal Rate, Portfolio Composition, and Payout Period in Which Withdrawals Are Adjusted for Inflation | | | | | | | | | | |
|---|---|---|---|---|---|---|---|---|---|---|
| | Annualized Withdrawal Rate as a Percentage of Initial Portfolio Value | | | | | | | | | |
| Payout Period | 3% | 4% | 5% | 6% | 7% | 8% | 9% | 10% | 11% | 12% |
| 100% Stocks | | | | | | | | | | |
| 15 Years | 100% | 100% | 100% | 94% | 86% | 76% | 71% | 64% | 51% | 46% |
| 20 Years | 100% | 100% | 92% | 80% | 72% | 65% | 52% | 45% | 38% | 25% |
| 25 Years | 100% | 100% | 88% | 75% | 63% | 50% | 42% | 33% | 27% | 17% |
| 30 Years | 100% | 98% | 80% | 62% | 55% | 44% | 33% | 27% | 15% | 5% |
| 75% Stocks/25% Bonds | | | | | | | | | | |
| 15 Years | 100% | 100% | 100% | 97% | 87% | 77% | 70% | 56% | 47% | 30% |
| 20 Years | 100% | 100% | 95% | 80% | 72% | 60% | 49% | 31% | 25% | 11% |
| 25 Years | 100% | 100% | 87% | 70% | 58% | 42% | 32% | 20% | 10% | 3% |
| 30 Years | 100% | 100% | 82% | 60% | 45% | 35% | 13% | 5% | 0% | 0% |
| 50% Stocks/50% Bonds | | | | | | | | | | |
| 15 Years | 100% | 100% | 100% | 99% | 84% | 71% | 61% | 44% | 34% | 21% |
| 20 Years | 100% | 100% | 94% | 80% | 63% | 43% | 31% | 23% | 8% | 6% |
| 25 Years | 100% | 100% | 83% | 60% | 42% | 23% | 13% | 8% | 7% | 2% |
| 30 Years | 100% | 96% | 67% | 51% | 22% | 9% | 0% | 0% | 0% | 0% |
| 25% Stocks/75% Bonds | | | | | | | | | | |
| 15 Years | 100% | 100% | 100% | 99% | 77% | 59% | 43% | 34% | 26% | 13% |
| 20 Years | 100% | 100% | 82% | 52% | 26% | 14% | 9% | 3% | 0% | 0% |
| 25 Years | 100% | 95% | 58% | 32% | 25% | 15% | 8% | 7% | 2% | 2% |
| 30 Years | 100% | 80% | 31% | 22% | 7% | 0% | 0% | 0% | 0% | 0% |
| 100% Bonds | | | | | | | | | | |
| 15 Years | 100% | 100% | 100% | 81% | 54% | 37% | 34% | 27% | 19% | 10% |
| 20 Years | 100% | 97% | 65% | 37% | 29% | 28% | 17% | 8% | 2% | 2% |
| 25 Years | 100% | 62% | 33% | 23% | 18% | 8% | 8% | 2% | 2% | 0% |
| 30 Years | 84% | 35% | 22% | 11% | 2% | 0% | 0% | 0% | 0% | 0% |

Note: Data for stock returns are monthly total returns to the S&P 500 Index, and bond returns are total monthly returns to high-grade corporate bonds. Both sets of returns data are from Jan 1926 to Dec 2009 as published by Morningstar. Inflation adjustments were calculated using annual values of the CPI-U. Table used with permission of the study authors.

**Table 2**

**Immediate Annuities**

Another method of converting wealth to income is to look at the current rate being offered on an immediate annuity. In general, I'm not a big fan of annuities, but I make an exception for a single premium immediate annuity (SPIA). The concept of a SPIA is very simple. You give a lump sum of money to an insurance company. In return, the insurance company will give you a guaranteed income for the rest of your life. In November 2013, immediate annuities could be purchased at the rates shown in Table 3.

This table demonstrates that if you're willing to give up control of the principal (remember that unlike a typical investment, there is nothing left of an immediate annuity when you die), you can convert wealth to income at a higher rate. A person retiring at seventy can use a million dollar portfolio to buy an inflation-indexed annuity that will pay $63,800 per year for the rest of his life. The point remains that if you think you can spend 10% or more of your portfolio each year in retirement, you'd best not start spending until you are either relatively old or relatively sick.

| Age | Annuity Payout | Inflation Adjusted Annuity Payout | Life Expectancy |
|---|---|---|---|
| 40 | 4.90% | 2.77% | 38 years |
| 50 | 5.56% | 3.47% | 29 years |
| 60 | 6.49% | 4.49% | 21 years |
| 70 | 8.28% | 6.38% | 14 years |
| 80 | 11.38% | 9.60% | 8 years |

**Table 3**

**The Millionaire Next Door**

Perhaps the most important book about millionaires in the popular finance literature of the last twenty years is *The Millionaire Next Door* by Thomas Staley and William Danko. This book, published in 1996, distilled the wisdom acquired from Stanley and Danko's academic studies about who the millionaires in America really are. Eighty percent of American millionaires are "first generation rich." In fact, the prototypical millionaire in their studies was fifty-seven years old, married with three children, and had a median income of only $131,000 per year (remember, the book was published in 1996).

The majority are self-employed business owners/entrepreneurs in a "dull-normal" profession, such as welding or paving contractors, dry cleaning, farmers, or mobile home park owners. They generally consider themselves to be "very frugal" but consider their spouse to be even more frugal than they are. On average, they've never paid more than $400 for a suit, $140 for a pair of shoes, $235 for a watch, or $29,000 for a car. Their most popular cars are Ford F-150s and Ford Explorers, and more than a third of them still buy them used. Most of them budget, and those who don't "pay themselves first" (by prioritizing retirement and other savings) before spending the rest rather than saving what is left at the end of the month. In short, Stanley and Danko found that millionaires don't look like millionaires. It turns out it is very hard to both "live like a millionaire" and "be a millionaire." The lesson of *The Millionaire Next Door* is this:

*"Most people have it all wrong about wealth in America. Wealth is not the same as income. If you make a good income each year and spend it all, you are not getting wealthier. You are just living high. Wealth is what you accumulate, not what you spend....It is seldom luck or inheritance or advanced degrees or even intelligence that enables people to amass fortunes. Wealth is more often a result of a lifestyle of hard work, perseverance, planning, and most of all, self-discipline."*

### Dr. North and Dr. South

In one of the great paradoxes of the book, we learn that physicians are, given their relatively high income, horribly underrepresented among the ranks of the wealthy. That fact seems hard to believe if wealth is really the result of hard work, perseverance, planning, and self-discipline. Nobody gets into, much less through, even the easiest of residencies without those four qualities. So why aren't more doctors rich?

Stanley and Danko dedicate an entire chapter of their book to a discussion of the frugal Dr. North and the spendthrift Dr. South. Both are highly paid specialists earning $700,000 a year who are in the later years of their careers. Dr. North has a net worth of $7.5 million. Dr. South has a net worth of just $400,000. The difference between them can best be summed up by looking at some of their annual expenditures in Table 4.

| Consumption Category | Annual Spending | |
|---|---|---|
| | Dr. North | Dr. South |
| Clothing | $8,700 | $30,000 |
| Motor Vehicles | $12,000 | $72,200 |
| Mortgage | $14,600 | $107,000 |
| Club Dues and Expenses | $8,000 | $47,900 |

**Table 4**

I remember a lunchtime talk presented to our class in medical school by a financial adviser who happened to be married to a family practitioner. His opening slide presented an ophthalmologist who was earning $350,000 a year and spending $400,000 a year. I resolved right then that I was going to live on far less than my gross income. Thirteen years ago I thought it was insane for anyone to be spending so much money in a single year. I understand much better now how easy it is to blow through several hundred thousand dollars in a single year. It really is the same game whether you make $40,000 or $400,000 a year. Stanley and Danko found that millionaires not only live below their means, but also they live WELL BELOW their means. So do I, and that's how I became a millionaire at thirty-eight. If you do the same, you'll find similar financial success.

### Reasons Why Physicians Are UAWs

Stanley and Danko classified people into two categories—under accumulators of wealth (UAW) or prodigious accumulators of wealth (PAW)—based on a simple formula: multiply your age by your annual income and divide by ten. If the result is more than your net worth, you're a UAW. If the result is less than your net worth, you're a PAW. This formula has some value for most people but very little value for a doctor due to the large investment of time and money required to become a practicing physician. Consider a doctor who comes out of residency at thirty. He did everything right in medical school and kept his loans to just $150,000. He now has a starting salary of $250,000. According to Stanley and Danko, his net worth should be $750,000. Instead, his net worth of negative $150,000 tags him as a UAW. In reality, he is doing quite well compared with his peers.

As an aside, the definition of financial success shouldn't have anything to do with how much other people have but rather on whether or not you are on track to meet your own financial goals. Despite reaching millionaire status just seven years out of residency, the formula also classifies me as a UAW, and I seem to be doing quite well, both when compared with my peers and my own financial goals. I developed a different rule that seems to fit physicians much better The formula, like any rule of thumb, isn't perfect, but it is a lot more useful for doctors and similar professionals.

# Physician Net Worth Rule

Expected Physician Net Worth (EPNW) =
Salary X Years in Practice X 0.3 – $200,000

Table 5 demonstrates my physician net worth rule in an example. This physician came out of residency with a salary of $250,000, which grew rapidly to $300,000 in the first couple of years, and then gradually increased at about the rate of inflation.

| Year | Salary | EPNW |
|------|--------|------|
| 0 | $250,000 | -$200,000 |
| 1 | $275,000 | -$117,500 |
| 2 | $300,000 | -$20,000 |
| 3 | $309,000 | $78,100 |
| 4 | $318,270 | $181,924 |
| 5 | $327,818 | $291,727 |
| 6 | $337,65 | $407,775 |
| 7 | $347,782 | $530,343 |
| 10 | $358,216 | $874,647 |
| 15 | $368,962 | $1,460,330 |
| 20 | $380,031 | $2,080,186 |
| 25 | $391,432 | $2,735,740 |
| 30 | $403,175 | $3,428,574 |

**Table 5**

His expected net worth at residency graduation is MINUS $200,000. His net worth should turn positive by post-residency year three, and hit $1 million after eleven years. At post-residency year thirty, typical retirement age, he should have a net worth of over $3 million. At post-residency year five, if his net worth were $200,000, he would be a UAW. If he had $2,000,000, at year fifteen, he would be a PAW.

## Seven Reasons Physicians Do Not Accumulate Wealth

Despite the uselessness of Stanley and Danko's formula for physicians, their research was clear that physicians do not tend to be wealth accumulators for seven reasons.

**First,** among those earning more than $100,000, there is, surprisingly, a negative correlation between education and wealth. PAWs are LESS likely than UAWs to hold advanced degrees. The reason why is not entirely clear, but may be due to the late start to earning and saving caused by extended periods of time in higher education.

**Second,** there is a bit of a lottery effect among entrepreneurs who start their own businesses. Business owners simply don't become successful enough to earn more than $100,000 a year unless they have established the same habits that will cause them to be a PAW. The same habits that cause them to be successful in their business lives lead them to success in their personal financial lives. In contrast, physicians, like athletes and artists, don't necessarily need to be good with money to earn a high income.

**Third,** physicians and other highly educated professionals simply get a late start. A physician who goes straight through from high school to college to medical school to residency comes out of training at age twenty-nine at the very earliest and more typically in his early to mid-thirties. When compared with his college roommate who took his first paying job at twenty-two, a physician who comes out of training at thirty-two may be seven to eleven years behind in earnings and savings. This, of course, ignores the fact that to some college graduates a resident's salary looks pretty good, in which case the physician is really only four years behind. To make matters worse, he begins much further behind the starting line due to the ever-increasing costs of his education.

If you compared the earnings/savings race between a physician and his college roommate to a 400-yard dash, the physician might be the faster runner, but he has to start fifty yards behind the starting line (student loans), he has to give his roommate a 15-second head start (lost earning years), and he has to run with a parachute tied to his waist (higher tax burden). It turns out the doctor has to be REALLY FAST (high earner with a very high savings rate) to still win.

**Fourth,** doctors are afflicted with the status placed upon them by society. Nobody expects a dry cleaning store owner to be living in a nice neighborhood and driving a Jaguar, but every attending physician has at least one friend, family member, or neighbor who refers to him as "that rich doctor." Society will judge a book by its cover whether people like it or not. People judge a doctor, a lawyer, or other professional by their outward appearance. If they live in a lousy neighborhood, drive a beater, or dress in less-expensive clothes, the assumption may be made that they are not good at their profession. I suspect this concern is larger in the minds of the professional than it is in the minds of those who patronize their services, but the end result is the same. Stanley and Danko state, "As a rule, doctors have an exceptionally high level of domestic overhead. The concern in many of these households is with consuming, not investing."

**Fifth,** doctors, especially those displaying a high lifestyle, are targeted by financial professionals, particularly those better described as financial "salespeople." Even nonfinancial professionals are more likely to charge a higher "doctor price" once they see your "School of Medicine" license plate holder but not nearly to the same extent as insurance agents, stockbrokers, and mutual fund salespeople. I can't believe how many financial "advisors" there are who "specialize" in physicians. They often have little knowledge of physician-specific financial issues but are experts at marketing to physicians. These unscrupulous salespeople often lead physicians into expensive, unwise investments. Once the physician has been burned a few times, they may try to invest on their own without actually learning anything about investing. This may lead them to take too much risk, such as gambling on individual stocks, day trading, or trying their luck in the options, currencies, or commodities markets. It can also lead doctors to invest too conservatively, such as using only money market funds or CDs, retarding their accumulation of wealth. Sometimes, it causes doctors not to invest at all, figuring they might as well enjoy their money now and let tomorrow "take care of itself."

**Sixth,** doctors tend to be charitable people. They weren't lying on their med school essays when they said, "I just really want to help people." Stanley and Danko found that PAWs were far more likely than most physicians to consider themselves as their favorite charity. I'm personally a big fan of supporting worthwhile charities, but there's no doubt that a dollar given to charity is a dollar that isn't going toward building wealth.

**Seventh,** doctors are busy people who are focused on important issues of life, death, and health. They work a lot of hours helping patients and their families make life-changing decisions. Boring, but necessary tasks, such as budgeting, meeting with advisors, and planning for their own financial future, often fall to the wayside.

You'll need to overcome these factors if you hope to become a millionaire, much less a millionaire by age forty. There are far too many physicians in their fifties with a net worth of under a million dollars. The habits that will help you avoid this fate need to be established as early as possible but at a minimum by the time you finish residency.

**Summary of Chapter 3**

- A million dollars isn't that much money anymore.
- $1 million really only supports an income of $30,000–$60,000 per year.
- Physicians are, in general, very poor at converting a high income into a high net worth.
- Millionaires are far more frugal than society imagines.
- Physicians may start out their career with a negative net worth but should still be able to retire as multimillionaires.

**Recommended Additional Reading**

Stanley, T. J., and Danko, W. D. (1996) *The Millionaire Next Door*. New York, NY: Pocket Books.

Doroghazi, R.M. (2006) *The Physician's Guide To Investing*. Totowa, NJ: Humana Press.

http://whitecoatinvestor.com/a-net-worth-rule-of-thumb-for-doctors/

http://whitecoatinvestor.com/the-physician-net-worth-rule-part-2/

# Chapter Four
# Medical School and Your Wealth

*"Although it is often stated 'invest in yourself,' it doesn't mean you should overspend or go into debt to pay for an education that you won't use.*
— Jeff Steiner, DO

Many decisions that you make as a premedical student and in medical school will have a dramatic effect on your ultimate ability to accumulate wealth and "live the good life." This chapter will examine each of these decisions and provide factors to consider when weighing them. Many readers of this book are certainly already through medical school and residency. Feel free to skip to the next chapter. Any financial errors you may have made as a premed or medical student are probably already "water under the bridge," although you might benefit from learning about the Public Service Loan Forgiveness (PSLF) program covered in this chapter.

## Be Careful Taking Time Off

I'm always surprised when I hear a premedical student who is planning to take an extra year as an undergraduate to "study for the MCAT" or "do more research" or "retake some of those science classes." Sometimes, they spend five years in college so that they can take a lighter load each semester, which will hopefully make it easier to earn an A in Organic Chemistry or Physics. Some people even do a master's degree or other post-baccalaureate program just to become a stronger applicant to medical school. Sometimes, people work as a paramedic, take a year off to travel, join the Peace Corps, or perhaps spend a little time in the business world. That's all fine if it is something you really want to do or if it is absolutely necessary in order for you to get into medical school. I took a couple of years off in college to be a missionary and do not consider a minute of it wasted. It made me a better person and a better doctor.

Prior to taking a significant amount of time off, you should consider the opportunity cost. The cost isn't just a year of your life. It is a year of "peak earnings" for whatever your eventual specialty might be. For example, if you are an orthopedist making $500,000 a year, those two years you spent working on a master's degree in chemistry would have an opportunity cost of a million dollars!

I find that people taking time off just to boost their application are usually doing so due to a lack of confidence, a lack of planning, or simply because they did a lousy job applying to medical school. Some are simply poor medical school applicants due to a lack of hard work, a lack of intelligence, or an inability to commit the necessary time and resources to the process for whatever reason. Many of those people will never get into, much less through, the medical education pipeline. But for those who do, that extra year or two can be very costly.

Of course, if you are not sure that medicine is for you, it would be a colossal mistake to go to medical school at all. The opportunity cost of a lost year or two deciding pales in comparison to losing a decade in education and training plus a decade paying back the loans for that education.

This principle also applies to those already in medical school or even residency. Sometimes, we become professional students, forgetting that at some point we've got to get out and get a return on our educational investment. I met one of the best doctors I know when I was a resident and he was an MS2. He spent four years in college, two years as a missionary, four years in medical school, a year in an MPH program, five years in a surgery residency, a year in a burn fellowship, and a year in a trauma fellowship. He will come out of training soon at age thirty-six. He's a fantastic doctor, but he will not be a millionaire at forty.

Many decisions you will be faced with as a medical student have financial ramifications. An MD/PhD is great for someone who wants to make research a big part of his career. But that extra three to five years of lost earnings probably isn't doing you any favors if you end up being a community neurologist instead of a researcher, even if you include the stipend and tuition credits offered in the program. Internal medicine, pediatric, and emergency medicine subspecialists are often in the same boat. I think it is wonderful that there are people out there willing to be endocrinologists, pediatric rheumatologists, and toxicologists. These specialties certainly pay enough that their practitioners can eventually reach financial security. The road to success, however, will be longer than for other specialties with a higher ratio of salary to years of training required.

Perhaps the dilemma is best illustrated in my own field of emergency medicine. Consider an emergency physician who decides to become a pediatric emergency doc. He spends two more years in training and then makes LESS money than his residency classmates. In emergency medicine, there is also an interesting phenomenon where some residencies last four years, but most take three years. That fourth year might help you land a job in academia (although most academic jobs seem to prefer a 3-year residency and a 1-year fellowship), but you certainly won't be offered any more money to join a community emergency medicine group. That last year of residency is essentially a year of lost earnings. Money isn't everything, but to pretend it doesn't matter at all is probably a mistake.

## Applying To Medical School

While the remainder of this chapter will have little relevance for a practicing physician, decisions made as a premedical student can have a profound impact on a physician's eventual financial situation. I'll include a few sections here for the premedical student in hopes that they can get this information prior to making those critical decisions.

Many people end up losing a year or two simply because they do not know how to apply to medical school. This is not very hard, but some applicants do not get good advice on how to do it well. I spent some time as an MS4 on my medical school admissions committee and learned a lot about how to apply successfully to medical school. Submit your applications as early as possible. There is no doubt that the early bird gets the worm when it comes to medical school slots. You also need to make sure your application is perfect. I found it hard to believe how many grammar, punctuation, and spelling mistakes could be found in dozens of applications. How hard is it to run a spell-check and have your roommates and mother read your essay? Many medical school admissions committee members will find your lack of attention to detail a disqualifying condition.

Students often do not do a very good job choosing which schools to apply to. You should apply only to schools reasonably likely to accept you. This includes all the state schools in your state, state schools in other states that actually take large numbers of out-of-state students, and private schools that have taken students from your college in the past. You might have some "dream schools" but also include some "safety schools."

Medical school admissions statistics are widely available. It is not that hard to figure out which schools receive fewer applications and whose accepted students had lower average GPA and MCAT scores. While there is no doubt that the quality of education differs between schools, few would argue that a great student at a "mediocre school" won't become a great doctor. Besides, 90% of what you will need as a practicing physician will be learned in residency anyway. It is probably a mistake to pass up an admission to a less prestigious school this year in hopes of getting into a more prestigious one next year. Aside from the risk of not getting into the better school next year, there's the repeated application and interview expenses, possible additional loans for additional education, and most importantly, the lost year of "peak earnings."

The other mistake I see premedical students make is that they don't apply to enough schools. My medical school routinely had 300 solid applicants for our class of 100. Once you've demonstrated you're qualified, it really comes down to how interesting you are, and that by necessity has a bit of a "luck" aspect to it. It really is a numbers game. You need to apply to enough schools that you get enough interviews that you get into at least one school. That's going to be ten schools for the best applicants, fifteen for the average applicant, and perhaps twenty to thirty or more for a mediocre applicant Sure, that might be a few thousand dollars in application fees, but that money will pale in comparison to a year of lost earnings. Besides, you can always turn down interviews if you get too many. Spending a few hundred dollars too much sure beats sitting around for a year and going through the process again.

## How to Choose a Medical School

So now you've applied to fifteen schools and went on seven interviews. Congratulations, you've been accepted to three different schools! How do you choose between them? That's easy. Go to the cheapest one. While there are some small differences in quality from one school to another, there is pretty much zero correlation between the price of the school and the quality of the education. If you can get into your state medical school, that is almost surely the best choice for you. Very few of your patients will care where you went to medical school. Except for prestigious academic positions, your future employers will care very little. The quality of your residency and fellowship training will be far more important to most people. Even residency directors do not care about the name of your school as much as your board scores, letters of recommendations, and rotation grades, especially in your chosen specialty. Medical education is pretty standardized, and everyone takes the same USMLE and/or COMLEX exams, studies from the same books, and holds the same retractors in the OR. You may want to spend a little more money in order to be in a desirable city or to go to a school where you think the education will be better. But don't spend a lot more. Certainly don't spend twice as much.

## Figure Out How to Pay For School

There are many ways to pay for medical school. By far the best is to spend the money you or your parents saved up to pay for your education. What? That's not an option? You could take out a few hundred thousand dollars in high interest loans. Not interested in that either? Well, there are some other options.

## MD/PhD Programs

The first option is to enroll in an MD/PhD or DO/PhD program. In return for committing to get the PhD, you not only get free tuition, but you also get a living stipend each year. These programs are fantastic options for someone who actually wants to get an MD AND a PhD. Unfortunately, there are a lot fewer students qualified to attend medical school who want an MD and a PhD than there are MD/PhD slots available. But these slots do not go unfilled. They are filled either by students who cannot get into the regular MD program or by students who do not really want that PhD but do not want to borrow hundreds of thousands of dollars to pay for medical school. Sure, they will all convince themselves they really do want the PhD, but take a look at their faces as they head off to the lab for four to five years when you head off to the wards as an MS3. Do they really look that excited?

I think a reasonable goal is to finish your training before your children start college. MD/PhD students are often cutting it pretty close. If your statistics do not look so good, you might find that some MD/PhD programs are a little more lenient than the straight MD program. Just like spending an extra year or two buffing up an application, I would only go this route if I absolutely had to. Being a slave for four years as a resident is bad enough. Doing it twice might be unbearable if you're not really into doing research.

## Join the Military

The military offers the Health Professions Scholarship Program (HPSP). This program pays your tuition, mandatory fees, a monthly stipend (around $2,000 per month), and even a $20,000 signing bonus. This is the method I used to pay for medical school. I discovered that there are many unhappy doctors in the military who discovered, only too late, that this "scholarship" isn't a scholarship in any reasonable sense of the word. Yes, they pay for medical school. But then they pay you far less than you would otherwise be worth. For example, in my specialty of emergency medicine, a military doctor makes about $120,000 a year. In the civilian world, a board certified emergency doctor can make two or even three times that amount. The difference is even higher for more highly reimbursed specialists since military pay is based more on rank and years of service than your specialty. The military orthopedists I worked with were only making $10,000–$20,000 a year more than I was.

The biggest issue with the HPSP scholarship is that those who take it are forced to go through the military match, which is completely different from the civilian match. Those who desire highly competitive specialties or who don't excel in medical school often find themselves paying back their military time with only a single year of internship and then have to return to residency upon completion of their military service. Just as an MD/PhD program is a great option for someone who wants to spend a career in research, the HPSP program is a great option for someone who actually wants to be a military doctor. If you're just looking for a way to pay for medical school, steer clear. As tuition skyrockets, loan terms worsen, and physician reimbursement decreases, the HPSP is becoming a better option than it used to be, but I once ran the numbers and discovered I came out $180,000 behind by taking that scholarship. I loved many things about serving my country, but I'm not sure it was worth paying $180,000 for the experience.

Those with prior military service desiring low-paying specialties, such as family practice or pediatrics, who are attending expensive medical schools are those most likely to benefit financially from the HPSP program. The military offers several programs besides the HPSP scholarship. Uniformed Services University of the Health Sciences (USUHS,) the military medical school, carries a 7-year commitment to the military instead of just four years but pays you more as you attend. The Financial Assistance Program (FAP) pays you less than the HPSP program but allows you to avoid the military match because you do not enroll until you are a resident. There are significant signing bonuses for attending physicians who want to join the military. The National Guard also offers a program for certain specialties.

## National Health Service Corps

The National Health Service Corp (NHSC) also offers a scholarship with some similarities to the military. While you can avoid the vagaries of the military match and being deployed to war zones, you'll still earn a relatively low salary and have limited control over where you live while paying your time back. The program is really aimed at getting primary care physicians into such underserved areas as rural towns and inner cities. The NHSC will only take the following specialties: Family Medicine, Internal Medicine, Pediatrics,

Geriatrics, Psychiatry, and Obstetrics/Gynecology. You apply during your fourth year of medical school and are then committed for three years after residency. In return for that commitment, you will receive a maximum of $120,000 toward student loan payback. In my opinion, this is a terrible deal unless the salary offered is very similar to what you would get for a non-NHSC position (unlikely) or you wish to practice in a qualifying community anyway.

## Loan Payback

Many towns and hospitals have a difficult time recruiting physicians of different specialties to their town and are willing to offer loan payback programs in order to attract them. These are most common for primary care specialties but can also be seen for emergency doctors, surgeons, and other specialists. There's usually a reason these hospitals need to wave some dollars in front of your nose to get you to come there. It may be because the hospital is dysfunctional, the patient population is unpleasant, the workload is high, or, more likely, because it is located in a rural area unattractive to professionals. But if you want to live in this town anyway, it can be a great deal.

## Public Service Loan Forgiveness

The Public Service Loan Forgiveness may allow many physicians to have hundreds of thousands of dollars in loans forgiven in the future. I say "may" because the program is so new and takes so long (ten years after medical school) that no physicians have actually had their loans forgiven yet. There are three keys to this program.

The **first key** is to pay as little as possible toward your loans for ten years. This is done using the Income Based Repayment (IBR) program or its new, improved version the Income Contingent Repayment (ICR) program. Under this program, your student loan payments are based on your income rather than how much you owe or the interest rate on the loans. As a general rule, residents and fellows in the IBR program are making lower payments and then once they get out of training they are making their regular payments (which are amortized over a 10-year period). After ten years of making payments, the remainder is forgiven. Your IBR payments are set at 10% of your "disposable income." Lower taxable income results in lower payments and thus more money that can be forgiven. For this reason, if you have a working spouse, you may wish to file your taxes as "Married Filing Separately" while in residency. You may also wish to take advantage of tax-deferred savings opportunities to further lower your taxable income.

For a typical physician, the amount of loans that can be forgiven is the sum of the difference between your "full" payments and the lower IBR payments you made while in training. If you owed $200,000 at 6.8%, a 10-year payment plan would require you to pay $2,302 per month. If instead you made $300 per month IBR payments for the five years you were in residency and then made the full $2,302 payments for the remaining five years, you would end up paying a total of $156,120 instead of $276,240— a savings of $120,120. A pulmonologist could have more forgiven due to his longer training period, and a family doctor would be eligible for much less, due to his shorter training period.

The **second key** is to work for a qualifying employer, generally a nonprofit or government employer. Fortunately, most residency and fellowship programs are at qualifying 501(c)3 hospitals. After training, you must also seek employment with a 501(c)3 hospital or other employer (not j ust a group that contracts with the hospital.) A physician who spends five to six years in training may have more than half of his student loans forgiven.

The **third key** is to make sure as much of your loan burden as possible is composed of direct loans from the federal government (Stafford and Direct Plus). Private loans and refinanced loans are not eligible for forgiveness. Credit card loans, auto loans, home equity loans, parental loans, and other creative ways to pay for school are also not eligible.

### Borrowed Money

Even with all these different programs out there, the vast majority of medical students are still going to go the traditional route of borrowing money to pay for medical school and paying it back as an attending. You can still get out of debt in four years like your classmates in the MD/PhD, HPSP, NHSC, and PSLF programs. You just have to pretend you have an income like your classmates and direct the remainder of your salary to debt repayment. If you are making $250,000 and living on $120,000 like your HPSP classmates and directing the balance of your salary toward your student loans, you should still have them paid off in just two to five years.

## Be a Poor Medical Student

It is far easier to be young and poor than to be old and poor. When you are in medical school, nearly everyone you associate with is young and poor. For a medical student, "keeping up with the Joneses" means driving a beater instead of taking the bus and drinking Sam Adams instead of Budweiser. It is a great time to learn how to budget and live frugally. It will be the same drill later as your income grows as a resident and then again as an attending, just with more zeros. If you can't live within a reasonable budget as a student, you'll find yourself taking out more loans as a resident and growing rapidly into your entire income as an attending. This is a certain recipe for financial disaster.

It might help the medical student struggling with being frugal to consider the ultimate cost of everything he buys with borrowed money. Remember that $10,000 borrowed at 7.9% as an MS1 will be $19,824 by the time he finishes a surgical residency and as much as $42,404 by the time it is paid off. Whenever you think you need that new pantsuit or a vacation to Tahiti, remember that the price (for you) is really two to four times as much as the tag says. N. Eldon Tanner, a Canadian businessman and later a Mormon leader during the Great Depression, summed it up well when he described just how hard interest works against you.

> *"Interest never sleeps nor sickens nor dies; it never goes to the hospital; it works on Sundays and holidays; it never takes a vacation; it never visits nor travels; it takes no pleasure; it is never laid off work nor discharged from employment; it never works on reduced hours; it never has short crops nor droughts; it never pays taxes; it buys no food; it wears no clothes; it is unhoused and without home and so has no repairs, no replacements, no shingling, plumbing, painting, or whitewashing; it has neither wife, children, father, mother, nor kinfolk to watch over and care for; it has no expense of living; it has neither weddings nor births nor deaths; it has no love, no sympathy; it is as hard and soulless as a granite cliff. Once in debt, interest is your companion every minute of the day and night; you cannot shun it or slip away from it; you cannot dismiss it; it yields neither to entreaties, demands, or orders; and whenever you get in its way or cross its course or fail to meet its demands, it crushes you.*

## Choose the Right Specialty

Doctors are generally very idealistic people and never more so than when they are in medical school. Most doctors truly did go to medical school out of a desire to help people rather than to seek a financially comfortable life. As a result, they generally do not put enough emphasis on either salary or lifestyle when choosing their specialty. The most important factor, of course, is to choose work you will enjoy for countless hours each year for the next several decades. You are far better off being a pediatrician for thirty years than burning out as a general surgeon after a decade. However, the second most important factor, and one that will become increasingly important to you as time goes on, is the salary and lifestyle associated with that specialty. With the possible exception of your choice of spouse, your choice of specialty will have a larger effect on your future income, wealth, and control over your lifestyle than any other decision made in those four years. There is a reason that dermatology is so competitive in the match. Its practitioners are routinely the happiest physicians in surveys. The specialty offers good pay, a great lifestyle, a low burnout rate, and a relatively short training period. Personally, I would hate going to work every day in a dermatology clinic, but if I didn't, that would have been a fantastic specialty choice.

Now, don't get me wrong, I'm very grateful to those physicians who choose low-paying specialties with long years of training. I'm also grateful to the gastroenterologists and surgeons who pick up the phone at 11 p.m. to come in and pull steak out of esophaguses and appendices out of bellies. It takes all types to provide good medical care. Most medical students eventually become dead set on a specialty long before the time they apply for the match in the fall of their fourth year. However, many medical students would feel fulfilled and happy practicing more than one specialty. If that is you, choose the one with the better salary and lifestyle.

I remember my own decision late in my third year of school. I had unexpectedly loved my OB/GYN rotation. I had entered medical school thinking I would be a family doctor but changed direction after meeting some emergency docs as an MS2 and enjoying my first Emergency Medicine (EM) rotation late in my third year. So there I was, choosing between OB/GYN and EM. I loved the work equally. EM appealed to my desire for breadth and procedures and fit my "ADHD Personality." OB/GYNs split their time between clinic, the OR, and the labor deck, and that's where the only patients happy to be in the hospital are located. I thought I could really enjoy a career doing some laparoscopic surgery in between crash C-sections. I truly loved both equally. So I decided to take salary and lifestyle into consideration. There were no EM residents at my hospital at the time, but the OB/GYN residents looked pretty miserable. I was working over 100 hours as a student on the service, and the residents were there more than I was. To make matters worse, the attendings were there too.

The EM attendings were there in the middle of the night also, but at least they went home at 7 a.m. instead of to a full day of clinic. They didn't carry pagers, they trained for one year less, and they made a similar salary for half the number of hours at work. Once I combined my professional interests with my lifestyle and salary desires, the decision was clear. If you find yourself in a similar dilemma, choose the specialty with the better lifestyle and/or salary. I assure you it will matter a lot more to you in ten years than it does now. It is important to be happy at work, but part of being happy at work may be feeling you are being reimbursed adequately for the work you are doing and being able to balance work with family life and other interests. I would have been miserable at work AND at home if I had chosen OB/GYN. Instead, I have my dream job.

## Summary of Chapter 4

- Spending a decade becoming a doctor should also be considered from an investment perspective.
- Apply to medical school correctly the first time.
- In general, attend the least expensive medical school you can get into.
- Don't join the military, join the public health service, or embark on an MD/PhD program for financial reasons.
- Many doctors may qualify for loan forgiveness via the Public Service Loan Forgiveness (PSLF) program.
- If you do not qualify for PSLF, plan to pay your loans back within five years of residency graduation.
- Learn frugality as a medical student.
- When choosing a specialty, don't ignore lifestyle and income considerations.

**Recommended Additional Reading**

Anzalone, J. (2012) *What They Don't Teach You In Dental School.* Self-published via Bookbaby.

Rochlin, J., Simon, H. "Does Fellowship Pay: What Is The Long Term Financial Impact Of Fellowship Training In Pediatrics," Pediatrics 127 (2011):254-60.

http://www.aamc.org/cim/specialty/findyourfit/interests/

http://studentdoctor.net/2013/11/financial-considerations-for-the-student-doctor/

http://whitecoatinvestor.com/income-based-repayment/

http://whitecoatinvestor.com/how-much-can-you-get-forgiven-via-pslf/

http://whitecoatinvestor.com/refinance-your-medical-school-loans-at-a-lower-rate/

# Chapter Five
# Residency and Your Wealth

*"No one teaches you how to think about money in medical school or residency. Yet, from the moment you start practicing, you must think about it."* — Atul Gawande

There is a lot to learn in residency, and your chief concern should be learning how to be a great doctor. Your personal finances should not consume a great deal of your time and effort, but there are still a few things you need to make sure you do as a resident. If you have already graduated from residency, feel free to skip ahead to the next chapter. Many attending physicians, however, still don't save enough money, have an adequate emergency fund, or have a solid insurance plan. Those topics are all covered in this chapter.

## Learn to Save

If you're like most residents, this is the first time you've had a regular salary. If you haven't learned yet, it's time to learn to live on a budget. If that's too hard, practice the technique that even many millionaires use. Pay yourself first, and then spend the rest. The effect is the same in the end. There's no reason a resident needs to be living on borrowed money.

A typical resident makes $45,000–$50,000. That's exactly the same as the average household income in this country, and it is far above the poverty level. Is it easy to spend more than that? Absolutely. That's why the vast majority of Americans will never be millionaires, even those with six-figure incomes. If you're disciplined enough to study for a month for USMLE Step 1, then you're disciplined enough to live on $45,000.

I'm going to ask you to do one other thing. Instead of living on $45,000, live on $40,000. Impossible? Remember there's always someone down the street making a little less than you. Live like him and pocket the difference. There is no reason you cannot start building wealth in residency. Remember Figure 2 from the second chapter? Our net worth was slightly negative when we began residency, but by the end of 2006, the year I left residency, it was closing in on six figures. It is definitely easier to save money on an attending salary than on a resident salary but not that much easier. Same game, more zeros. The habits established matter more than the actual amount saved, but remember that the first dollars you save also have the longest amount of time for compound interest to work on them.

I never found saving or budgeting to be particularly difficult. I look at a budget as a "plan to achieve my financial goals" rather than some kind of limitation. The easiest way to start one is to simply write down what you spent last month (or next month if you cannot easily reconstruct a record). If your money is going where you want it to, then you don't have to do anything. For most people, however, there is a big disconnect between what they want and how they are actually spending their money. A budget is the process of realigning your behavior with what you actually want. Many physicians have found that using an online budgeting tool, such as Mint.com or You Need A Budget, is helpful to them when tracking their spending. Others can do it on a simple spreadsheet or even a piece of paper. If you really have a spending problem, you may have to go to a "cash in the envelopes" system where you withdraw your paycheck in cash, allot a certain amount to an envelope labeled "food," "rent," "entertainment," etc., and when the money is gone, it's gone.

### Try Not To Buy a House

There is an interesting phenomenon I've noticed among graduating medical students. They have been deferring gratification for so long that they have this incredible pent-up desire to "have a normal life" and "live the American dream." Combine this with heavy marketing from the real estate industry and it's no surprise that they all want to buy a house. Some are convinced that buying a house is the smart move financially, but most just have a subconscious idea that once they've bought a house, even if they own 0% of it, that they've made it. I know I'm not going to talk most residents out of buying a house. Most are going to buy a house no matter what I say. But at least consider the alternative—renting.

Renting doesn't necessarily mean living in a tiny apartment with messy roommates. You can rent condos, townhomes, starter homes, and luxury homes just like you can buy them. Buying IS a good financial move, once you're in a long-term, stable job situation. Residency might be stable, but it isn't long term. Your first job as an attending is often neither long term nor stable. It is okay to wait a few months to make sure the job is working out before buying. Besides, doing that is likely to get you a much better deal when you do buy a home.

There are exceptions to every rule, of course. The longer your training period and the more money your spouse makes, the better buying a house will work out. There are also rare situations where you cannot rent the home you need or desire and are forced to buy, but the general rule for a resident or fellow should be to rent your residence.

**Six Reasons Why Residents Should Not Buy a House**

1. The break-even period is same as residency length
2. A resident usually does not have a down payment
3. Tax breaks are not worth much to a resident
4. Owning a home is expensive
5. Attendings do not live in resident houses
6. Residents are busy

**1. The break-even period is the same as residency length**

Most calculations of a break-even period demonstrate that it typically takes three to five years just to break even when comparing buying with renting. That time period is amazingly similar to the length of residency. Which one works out better is just a coin flip. You might as well pick the one with the least hassle, which is definitely renting. There is less hassle getting in, less hassle maintaining it, and much less hassle getting out.

## 2. A resident usually does not have a down payment

You get a much better deal on a house when you bring a down payment of 20% of the price of the home. Most graduating medical students do not have the money to put toward a down payment. Sure, there are "physician's loans" out there that will loan you 100% of the value of the home AND the closing costs, allowing you to get into the home for virtually nothing. Ask the residents who bought a house in 2006 how that worked out for them. Not only do you lose the protection against a decline in value of your house that a down payment provides, but you also pay more in fees and a higher interest rate when you put less than 20% down. I've bought three houses in my life. The first, in 1999, with little to nothing down. It worked out poorly. The second, in 2006, with 20% down. It worked out okay, and considering the housing crash, very well. The last, in 2010 with 20% down, is working out great.

## 3. Tax breaks are not worth much

Realtors love to tout the tax benefits of buying a home, but the truth is that most residents get little to no tax benefit from buying a house. First, you have to have enough deductions that your itemized deductions are more than the standard deduction. The standard deduction in 2014 is $12,400. So, if your property taxes are $3,400, you need to be paying at least $9,000 a year in interest before any of it becomes deductible (less if you're paying significant income taxes or donating significant sums to charity). Given a 4% interest rate, $9,000 in interest in a given year indicates a loan value of $230,000. A loan of $230,000 plus property taxes of $2,800 a year and insurance of $600 a year means a monthly payment of $1,392, or about 37% of the typical resident's salary. Unless his spouse is making some decent money, a resident cannot afford that, much less enough more than that to actually create some significant tax breaks. Even if the resident can somehow find enough itemized deductions to beat the standard deduction, he is still in a very low tax bracket. Your tax break may be as little as 15% of the amount by which your itemized deductions exceed the standard deduction. Even if you manage to find $15,000 in standard deductions, that's only going to save you less than $500. One broken appliance is going to erase that. There are very real tax benefits available to homeowners, but the typical resident isn't going to see them.

## 4. Owning a home is expensive

Most first-time homeowners dramatically underestimate the costs of ownership, especially the transaction and maintenance costs. Plan on spending 5% of the value of the home to buy it, 10% to sell it, and 1%–2% a year to maintain it. On some occasions, you may get away with slightly less than this, but these are pretty good estimates. Too many first-time homebuyers compare the cost of the mortgage payment with the cost of the rent payment and forget about all the other costs of homeownership.

## 5. Attendings do not live in resident houses

Some residents mistakenly think they will live in the same house as an attending as they live in as a resident. While this may happen from time to time, it generally does not. It is hard to predict the future three to five years down the road, and many residents end up doing an unexpected fellowship or moving to another city to pursue a job opportunity. Children come along, requiring more bedrooms, and neither you nor your spouse are likely to be content for long living in a house you could afford on a salary of $50,000 when you're making $250,000.

## 6. Residents are busy

It not only costs money to buy, maintain, and sell a house, but it also costs time, which is an extremely valuable commodity for a resident. Do you really want to spend your two to four days off a month working on your fixer-upper? It feels awfully good to just sweep the floor and hand the keys to your landlord the day after residency graduation before driving out of town rather than trying to find a buyer or a renter for your house while trying to concentrate on your new life in another city. Being an "accidental landlord" (due to not being able to sell your property due to a bad market) from afar is neither pleasurable nor profitable, although it does beat paying two mortgages for an extended period of time. This is a situation many physicians have found themselves in recently.

## Start Insuring Against Financial Catastrophe

Perhaps the most important financial task to accomplish during residency is to buy some critical types of insurance. On your relatively small resident salary, the premiums for adequate disability, life, and liability insurance will seem very large to you. You should still purchase it. The consequences of your disability and death will rarely be higher than they are right at the beginning of your career.

Early in residency, buy as large of a high-quality, specialty-specific, own occupation, individual disability insurance policy as an agent is willing to sell you. The group disability policy offered by many hospitals and residency programs is less expensive, but provides less coverage and no longer covers you after graduation. A good individual disability policy for a resident will probably have a disability benefit of around $5,000 per month, or $60,000 per year. The cost will be 2%–5% of the benefit, or $1,200–$2,000 per year. Although a very expensive type of insurance, it is least expensive and most important while you are a resident. Unlike with many things in the financial world, with disability insurance, you tend to get what you pay for. If a particular policy is markedly cheaper, there is usually a reason. It's okay not to buy the most expensive policy available to you, but be sure you understand the differences between the various policies you are considering. Always purchase from an independent agent who can sell you a policy from many different companies. Ask if there are any discounts available on the policies presented. Sometimes a discount available through a medical association can decrease premiums by up to 30%. Residents should purchase cost of living riders, future purchase option riders, and residual disability riders. The cost of living and future purchase option riders are less important for disability insurance purchased by a mid- or late-career physician, but most disability policies should be purchased as a resident or young attending physician.

If you have someone besides you depending on your income, such as a spouse or children, you also need to buy a 20- to 30-year term, level-premium life insurance policy. This is a far easier task than buying disability insurance. There is little to compare between policies. Term life insurance is essentially a commodity, and by using an online service such asTerm4Sale, you can quickly compare prices. When you become an attending, you'll probably want a policy in the range of $2 million to $5 million. You might not want to spend that much as a resident, but at least buy $500,000 to $1 million. A healthy 27-year-old female can buy a $1 million 20-year level term policy for about $400 a year. A 30-year policy will run $550 a year. If you develop a significant chronic illness during your early thirties (not uncommon as you know), you may find you're uninsurable or insurable only at a very high rate by the time you graduate from residency.

Most residents quickly become aware of just how litigious our society has become. Your residency program will take care of your malpractice insurance, but you can also have very high liability from events that occur outside of work. Attending physicians should carry an "umbrella" policy with limits of $1 million to $5 million. A resident may not want to spend the $200 to $700 a year this type of policy costs, but at a minimum he should increase the liability limits on his auto and renter's/homeowner's policy to between $300,000 to $500,000.

### An Emergency Fund

An emergency fund is a pot of money consisting of three to six months' worth of your living expenses. It needs to last at least as long as your disability insurance waiting period, the length of time between the date you become disabled and the date when you start receiving payments from the insurance company. It should be invested in a very safe way. Perhaps some of it should be in cash at your home. It can be kept in your checking account, or if you'd like to earn a little more on it, in a savings account or a CD. There are two main purposes to an emergency fund. First, so that you never have to take on debt in the event of an emergency, such as job loss, a broken appliance, or a funeral on the other side of the country. Instead of putting those expenses on a credit card, you take the money out of your emergency fund. The second purpose of an emergency fund is to allow you and your family to worry much less about the fluctuation of value in your investments. Never worrying or fighting about money is an important part of living the good life.

### Residents Should Go Roth

Since you're now making money, it's time to start saving money. A Roth IRA (available to anyone) or Roth 401(k) or Roth 403(b) (available from your employer) is an ideal place for a resident to save money for retirement. Roth IRAs were instituted in 1997 by a law sponsored by Senator William Roth of

Delaware. Roth 401(k)s were instituted in 2010, and many 401(k)s have added this option to their plan. Instead of allowing pretax contributions like a traditional retirement account, such as a traditional IRA or 401(k), you contribute to a Roth IRA, Roth 401(k), or Roth 403(b) with after-tax dollars. The contributions grow in a tax-free manner just like tax-deferred retirement accounts, but upon withdrawal in retirement the money withdrawn is tax free. Since residents are generally in a lower tax bracket than they will be in for the rest of their career, and probably their retirement, it makes sense to pay the taxes up front. As a general rule, residents should contribute money to retirement accounts in the following order:

**Retirement Account Priority List for Residents**

1.  Roth 401(k)/403(b) up to the match provided by the employer
2.  Traditional 401(k)/403(b) (if no Roth option) up to the match provided by the employer
3.  Roth IRA up to the limit of $5,500 per year
4.  Spousal Roth IRA up to the limit of $5,500 per year
5.  Roth 401(k)/403(b) up to the $17,500 limit
6.  Traditional 401(k)/403(b) (if no Roth option) up to the $17,500 limit
7.  457 account

Most residents will struggle to save enough to max out one Roth IRA much less come up with $17,500 to max out a Roth 401(k). That's okay; the habit matters more than the amount of money.

### Learn About Finances

Physicians not only go through their twenties without making much money, they also do so without learning much about money. You've got some catching up to do. I recommend that just as a doctor does continuing medical education each year (CME), he should also do continuing financial education (CFE) each year.

At a minimum, force yourself to read one book on personal finance or investing each year of residency and throughout your career. I know it's dry, but so was nephrology as a MS2, and you learned that because you had to. Treat your CFE the same way. It's just part of your job to learn this information. Also pay attention to all of the aspects of contracting and billing that you may be exposed to. Pay special attention to the private attendings you come into contact with. Salaried academicians simply have much less exposure to and knowledge of these important subjects. Use the suggested books and websites listed after each chapter in this book to guide your study.

Residency is an awesome time that transforms you from a student to an experienced physician worthy of the trust of your patients and worthy of a high income. Your chief focus should be on learning medicine, but carving out just a little time to take care of a few financial chores and to learn about business, personal finance, and investing will pay huge dividends later.

## Summary of Chapter 5

- Your focus in residency should be on becoming a great doctor.
- Rent, don't buy, during residency.
- Buy a high-quality individual disability insurance policy.
- If someone else depends on you, buy a large life insurance policy.
- Start saving as a resident, preferably in a Roth IRA or Roth 401(k).

### Recommended Additional Reading

Steiner, J. (2013) *The Physician's Guide to Personal Finance:* Two Pugs Publishing.

http://term4sale.com

http://whitecoatinvestor.com/the-five-big-money-items-you-should-do-as-a-resident/

http://whitecoatinvestor.com/disability-insurance-introduction/

http://whitecoatinvestor.com/how-to-buy-life-insurance/

# Chapter Six
# The Secret to
# Becoming a Rich Doctor

*"If you do wish to splurge a little, to loosen up, do it after there is $1 million in the bank and after the mortgage has been paid."*
— Robert Doroghazi, MD, FACC

I'd much rather be a good physician than a rich one, but I don't see any reason why a doctor can't be both. Your patients, family, and friends all assume you're rich, so you might as well be rich. Medicine is a difficult career. It requires intelligence, perseverance, attention to detail, and a lot of hard work, and that's just to get into medical school.

Getting through the long pipeline requires even more of these attributes, many nights of lost sleep, and a decade of lost earnings. Even once you're out of training, you have to deal with constant liability, many more sleepless nights in many specialties, excessive government regulations, and the constant emotional drain of dealing with drug seekers, serious illness, death, and social catastrophes.

Although society at times almost makes you feel criminal for making a high income, the truth is that the vast majority of people agree that physicians should be highly paid for their work. Incomes may be trending down, but physicians are always going to be earning more than the average American household. Whether a doctor becomes wealthy with that high income, however, is entirely up to him and his family.

### Live Like a Resident

The most important year in a physician's financial life is his first year out of training, and the most important advice this book can give you is contained in just four words.

# Live Like A Resident!

Did you get that? I cannot emphasize it enough. You've just finished living on $40,000–$60,000 for three to five years. You know you can do it. The biggest single financial issue that most physicians face in their quest for "the good life" is the sudden quadrupling (at a minimum) of their income upon leaving residency. Too many doctors grow into this income much too quickly, often immediately. Those who aren't living on less than their income during residency often find they are actually spending more than their impressive salary within a year or two of residency completion. An even worse predicament happens to those residents who start building the staff physician lifestyle even before they graduate from residency by maxing out credit cards, getting high end car loans and a large mortgage in anticipation of the larger paycheck.

If a new attending physician can manage to live the same lifestyle he has been living as a resident, the vast majority of that additional income can be put toward increasing his wealth by paying for a significant down payment on a home, paying off student loans and other debt, and saving for retirement and other long-term goals. In addition, a graduating resident may be used to 80-hour workweeks. If he continues to work that hard in establishing his practice, he will not only enjoy an "attending income" but also a very high income for his specialty. This is not a very good long-term solution, as it can often lead to burnout and unhappiness, but doing it for a few years or even just a few months can really get you started off on the right foot in your new career.

Of course, this is very hard to do, and few new attendings honestly have the discipline to do it. I certainly didn't. Upon leaving residency, I entered a period of active duty with the US Air Force. My salary tripled from about $40,000 to about $120,000 a year. Did we live the same lifestyle we had as a resident? No. We had been renting a 2-room duplex for $800 a month in residency. Now we bought a 3-bedroom townhome for $138,000. We had just one cell phone between the two of us, so we bought another. We had been a one-car family, and we decided to get a second one (it literally cost $1,850.) Our lifestyle definitely improved, and it was wonderful. But it didn't triple. It probably didn't even double. Where did all that extra money go? First, it went to pay off a short-term loan my parents gave me to help with our down payment, but within a couple of months, we had a couple of thousand extra dollars every month that we had to decide what to do with. That's a great feeling. The money went into a 401(k), into Roth IRAs, toward paying down the mortgage, toward saving for the car we really wanted, toward college saving accounts for our children, and toward an emergency fund.

But there is a lot of room between living the same lifestyle you had as a resident and the lifestyle attainable by spending every cent of attending income. The slower you improve your lifestyle, the more wealth you will eventually attain. Moderation in all things, of course, but trust me when I say you'll still feel rich even if you only double your income instead of quadrupling it.

### That First Paycheck

At the end of July after you graduate from residency, someone is going to put $15,000–$45,000 into your bank account. Whether you ever become wealthy or not depends on what you decide to do with that first paycheck. Show me what happened to the money you made in your first year out of residency and I can predict your financial future with surprising accuracy.

Did you pay off all your consumer debt?
How much of it did you put toward retirement?
How much of your student loans did you pay off?
What are you now driving?
How much did you pay toward a mortgage?
What was your tax burden?

You might think you deserve to have a high income just because you went to medical school and completed residency, but you do not deserve to be wealthy unless you show you can carve out a significant chunk of that high income and put it toward building wealth. You've got a huge advantage over many of the millionaires profiled in *The Millionaire Next Door* who managed to get rich on a middle-class income of $50,000 to $100,000 a year. Don't blow it! It will be far easier for you to become wealthy than for them, but it still requires you to do a few things right, and the most important one is to not just live below your means but to live far below your means. An upper middle-class income combined with a middle-class lifestyle is a sure route to wealth. So is a "top 1%" income combined with an upper middle-class lifestyle.

## Location, Location, Location

Some of my favorite places in the world are in California. I love the beaches of San Diego, the High Sierras around Mt. Whitney, the walls of Yosemite, the deserts of Joshua Tree, the cool little mountain towns like Idyllwild and Mammoth and, when traffic and smog are not too bad, even its thriving cities. However, California is a toxic wasteland for physicians, particularly the big cities.

The pay may be slightly higher, but the cost of living is dramatically higher. A house that may cost $300,000 in Arizona, Nevada, or Utah could run as much as $3 million in parts of California. Combine the cost of living with poor Medi-Cal reimbursement, high state income taxes that are ridiculously progressive (the 9.3% bracket starts at less than $48,000) and competing with dot-com millionaires for housing in the best school districts, and it is easy to see that it will be difficult to get ahead as a doctor while practicing in the Bay Area. There are many similar places across the country on both coasts. You don't have to live there, and you will be much better off financially if you choose not to. States like Indiana and Texas offer low taxes, a low cost of living, a favorable medico-legal environment, and incomes comparable or even better than you'll find in California or Manhattan. You only live once, of course, and money isn't everything. If your entire family and everything you want to do is located in San Francisco, then you'll need to deal with the consequences of that. Just realize you'll be swimming upriver from a financial perspective.

## Get Your Family on the Same Page

In personal finance, there is little that is more important than you and your spouse being on the same page. The spouses of physicians have their own subculture and lore concerning the jump from resident to attending pay. Remember that they have been deferring gratification in anticipation of your residency graduation as much or more than you have. You may have even foolishly promised a new car, a big house, an unaffordable vacation, or an expensive piece of jewelry for that first year. It might not just be your spouse you need to convince of the merits of living like a resident. Many doctors have teenagers by the time they finish training, who are also ready to enjoy the fruits of your labors. It is important to start talking about your financial plans as far in advance as possible (preferably before marriage) so that there are no surprises for the other members of your family when your disposable income merely doubles upon residency graduation.

The benefits of growing into your income slowly are just as large for your family members as they will be for you. You don't need to be an extremist one way or the other. Moderation in all things. But following a solid financial plan should reduce the tension in your home around finances, not increase it. It also helps if you do not marry someone who views shopping as recreation or therapy.

## Ordering Your Priorities

I am often asked by physicians about what they should do first. These physicians are usually choosing between many good options, such as paying down debt, contributing to retirement accounts, or saving for a down payment. If you will live like a resident for your first few years in practice, you will find that you do not have to choose; you can actually do all of them at once through careful planning and budgeting. Consider a graduating resident with a salary of $250,000 and $200,000 in student loans. He may pay $50,000 in taxes, leaving him $200,000. If he can live on $75,000 per year (a 50% raise from his residency pay), he will still feel quite wealthy. He will then have $125,000 per year with which to build wealth. He may be able to contribute $17,500 to a 401(k), $5,500 to a Roth IRA, $5,500 to a spousal IRA, and another $6,550 to a Health Savings Account, for a total of $35,050 toward retirement. He can also put $50,000 toward his student loans and nearly $40,000 more toward the down payment on a house. By living like a resident, he can truly do it all. That said, I feel obligated to provide some guidelines to new attendings for allocating their income. A worthy goal for a new physician is that within five years of residency graduation the student loans will be paid off, the retirement nest egg will have caught up to those of your nonmedical peers, you will be living in your dream house, and you will be debt free except for a low interest rate, 15-year fixed mortgage.

## Develop a Housing Plan

The first priority is to develop a plan for your own housing. There are three approaches that are reasonable for a new attending. The first is to rent for a year or even two as an attending. This allows you to make sure you're a good fit for the job, boost your income, save up a 20% down payment, and get a great deal both on the house and on the mortgage.

The second approach is to use a "physician loan" to buy the dream house right out of residency. Although a physician loan will allow you to avoid the dreaded PMI (Private Mortgage Insurance simply insures the lender against your default on the loan), the fees and interest rate will be higher for a physician mortgage than a conventional 15-year fixed mortgage with 20% down. Instead of saving the down payment before buying a house, you would save it after buying the house by paying down the mortgage to the point where you could refinance it with a better mortgage. Alternatively, you could use the money that would have gone toward a down payment and put it toward the student loans or the nest egg. If you choose to use a physician mortgage, be sure you don't just fritter away the money that would have otherwise gone toward a 20% down payment.

The third option is to buy a "starter home" and save the down payment for the dream house within the starter home. This was the approach I took, since I knew I would be moving after four years anyway when I left the military. I wasn't able to come up with a down payment on a dream home quickly upon residency graduation, but I could scrape up enough to buy a little town home. We nearly had it paid off after four years and were able to take that home equity and use it as a down payment on the dream home. If you use this approach, you can either sell the starter home to get the equity, or you can take the equity out by refinancing and turn the starter home into an investment property.

## Develop a Student Loan Elimination Plan

The second priority is to determine a plan for your student loans. The two most common options with standard interest rate student loans (5%– 8%) are 1) to pay them off as soon as possible or 2) to pay the minimum due and get the rest forgiven through the Public Service Loan Forgiveness (PSLF) program. By the time you complete residency or fellowship and your Income Based Repayment (IBR) payments become the equivalent of regular payments, you should know if you are going to qualify for any forgiveness.

A third option, for those with very low interest student loans (1%–3%), such as those graduating from medical school in the early 2000s, is to stretch them out as long as possible, trying to arbitrage the rate by borrowing at 1%– 3% and investing at 5%–8%. There is additional risk in investing "on margin" like this, but it seems unlikely that over a long period of time a broadly diversified stock index fund will do worse than 3% per year, even after tax.

## Financial Priority List for Attending Physicians

Once you have developed a housing plan and a plan for your student loans, meld it into the following financial priority list for attending physicians.

1. **Get the match**. Employer-provided retirement plan matching funds are really part of your salary. Don't leave the match on the table by not contributing.
2. Pay off any **high-interest debt** (>8%), such as credit cards, car loans, expensive private student loans, etc. This is a fantastic guaranteed investment return.
3. Maximize your **tax-deferred retirement plan** contributions, including 401(k)s, profit-sharing plans, 403(b)s, 457s, and defined benefit/cash balance plans.
4. Fund a **Health Savings Account** (HSA) if eligible (more on these "Stealth IRAs" in chapter 8).

The following four items can be reordered, according to your financial priorities.

5.  Fund a personal and spousal **Backdoor Roth IRA** (more on this in chapter 8).
6.  Fund a **college savings plan** (529) for each child up to the amount that your state subsidizes with tax breaks.
7.  Pay off **moderate-interest debt** (4%–8%) such as student loans (unless you anticipate forgiveness).
8.  Save for a **house down payment** (if not using a physician loan).

The next four items can be reordered, according to your financial priorities and comfort level with debt.

9.  If you used a physician mortgage, pay it down to **enable refinancing** into a lower rate conventional mortgage.
10. Add additional funding if desired to **college savings** (529) accounts.
11. Invest in a **taxable account in risky investments** (stock index funds, real estate, etc.).
12. Pay off **low-interest (1%–3%) student loan** debt (unless you anticipate forgiveness).

The final three items can also be reordered according to your priorities.

13. Make **extra payments** on your mortgage.
14. Invest in a **taxable account in low-risk** investments (municipal bond funds, etc.).
15. **Spend your money** on what makes you happy.

If you follow this plan, then within just a few years of residency graduation, your student loans can be paid off, you can have a portfolio worth several hundred thousand dollars, and you should own at least 20%– 30% of your dream home with the remainder financed at a very low rate. At that point, put 20% of your income toward retirement and enjoy the rest of your money. Notice that the priority list doesn't include luxury cars, brand-new furniture, expensive trips, or other expensive motorized toys. There will be plenty of time and money to buy all these things. However, that time is after the student loans are gone, after you have a good-size nest egg, and after you own a good portion of your dream home. It is perfectly fine to have a few empty rooms in your dream home. You don't need to finance $50,000 in furniture and upgrades as soon as you move in. Buy them over time, paying cash.

The good life is not making payments on a mansion and two luxury cars upon residency graduation. The good life is having a job you love where you are making an important contribution to society. The good life is rebuilding relationships put on the back burner for the last decade. The good life is having thousands of dollars of unneeded income every month and getting to decide how you want to use it. You can use it to purchase financial freedom in the form of part-time work or early retirement; to pay for expensive toys, vacations, or a lake house; to send your children to an Ivy League college and grad school; to help your family; or to support your favorite charities. The good life is not only having your dream job but also being able to walk away from it if it stops being your dream job. The best way to do this is to live as much like a resident as you can for as long as you need to after finishing your training. Done properly, within just five years, most physicians can pay off all their loans, catch up to the retirement funds of their college roommates, and save a 20% down payment on their dream house. They can then be appropriately proud of both their professional and financial success.

**Summary of Chapter 6**

- Live like a resident until your student loans are gone.
- Grow into your salary slowly.
- Never grow into your salary completely.
- Work together with your family to ensure financial success.
- Deploy your income according to your priorities in order to get your dream house, pay off debt, and hatch a nest egg.

**Recommended Additional Reading**

Doroghazi, R.M. (2006) *The Physician's Guide to Investing*. Totowa, NJ: Humana Press.

http://whitecoatinvestor.com/10-reasons-why-residents-shouldnt-buy-a-house/

http://whitecoatinvestor.com/cost-of-living-matters-more-than-anything-else/

http://whitecoatinvestor.com/live-like-a-resident/

http://whitecoatinvestor.com/student-loans-vs-investing/

# Chapter Seven
# The Retirement Number YOU Control

*"Rather go to bed without dinner, than to rise in debt."*
— Benjamin Franklin

In the last chapter, I basically advised you to save as much as you can for as long as you can after residency by "living like a resident." For most doctors, that's a temporary plan. What's the point of being an attending if you're going to live like a resident for decades? The good life is not dying (or even retiring) with some huge stash of money. The goal is to have a nice life and to allow your finances to be a tool to help you generate happiness in yourself and those you care about.

The formula that dictates how much money you will end up with at retirement basically uses four variables—your income, what percentage of that income you save (your savings rate), the rate of return on your saved money, and the amount of time you allow that money to compound. While you do have some control over all of those numbers, the easiest to control is your savings rate. In this chapter, I'll demonstrate just how important this variable is to your wealth. But first, a demonstration of how these variables work together.

## The Four Variables at Work

Consider a physician who makes $200,000 per year, saves 10% of it from age thirty-one to age sixty-one, and compounds his money at 4% after inflation, investment expenses, and taxes. Using a financial calculator, or simply the Future Value function of a spreadsheet, we can see that at age sixty-one he'll have a portfolio of $1.6 million. Remember the 4% rule from chapter 3? If you apply it to $1.6 million, you'll see that you can support an income of more or less $64,000. Add in another $30,000 for Social Security and you'll see that this doctor will retire on an eventual income of about $94,000, or about 47% of his previous gross income. That will probably be a comfortable, but not an extravagant, retirement. Many financial advisors recommend you should aim to have 80% of your preretirement income in retirement, but that number is far too high for the typical physician. I'll explain more about that in a few pages.

But what if this doctor wants to retire at fifty-five instead with that same $94,000 income? Or if he wants to retire at sixty-one but didn't actually start saving until he was thirty-seven? How much more does he need to save to make up for that lost six years? It turns out he needs to save about $5,500 more a year, for a total of 13% of his income. If he wants to retire very early, such as at age fifty, that increases to about 18% of his income. If the doctor is okay with a full 30-year career but actually wants to replace 80% of his income in retirement (assuming the same $30,000 a year from Social Security), then it turns out he needs to save 24% of his income every year for thirty years, just for retirement.

It's easy to manipulate all of the numbers in this equation, and I recommend you spend a few minutes doing so with the spreadsheet on your computer. It will likely motivate you to save far more of your income than you may have been planning to save. The truth is that putting only 5%–10% of your gross income toward retirement probably isn't going to provide a very nice retirement. The right number is different for everyone, but likely lies in the 15%–25% range. I recommend doctors put 20% of their gross income toward retirement. If you are the rare doctor who gets into his fifties and finds he has oversaved a little, you can cut back then on your saving (or your working) or just plan on a more comfortable retirement. The truth is that almost no one oversaves, and early retirement will only be an option for those willing to dramatically pare back their lifestyle in retirement.

## The All-Important Savings Rate

In your first few years of investing, nothing matters more than your savings rate. Consider the doctor from the previous example who starts working and saving at age thirty-one. Which would have a larger effect on his net worth at forty—saving another 5% of his income or DOUBLING his investment return?

| Method | Net Worth At 40 |
|---|---|
| Saving 10%/Earning 4% | $220,122 |
| Saving 15%/Earning 4% | $330,183 |
| Saving 10%/Earning 8% | $269,731 |

**Table 6**

As you can see in Table 6, this physician would end up with 20% more net worth by saving just 5% more of his income than by doubling his investment return. Early in your investing career, there just isn't much money available to compound no matter how good your returns. It seems your portfolio has to get to a certain size before you're even "in the game," making money with money.

## The Worst News about Retirement

The biggest disappointment for those who are just learning about investing is to realize that the "mountain charts" that financial advisors love to show you don't represent reality. You know the charts I'm talking about. The advisor introduces it like this:

"This chart shows someone who invests $10,000 at age 20. Through the miracle of 12% compound interest, that $10,000 will grow to nearly $2.9 million by the time he retires at age 70!" Then he pulls out something that looks like Figure 4.

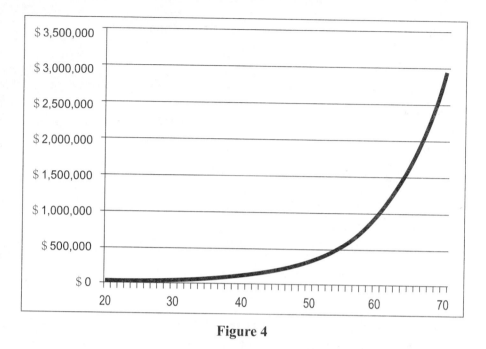

**Figure 4**

I'm sorry, but your money is absolutely NOT going to compound at 12%. In fact, it will likely compound at between 2% and 6%. That same $10,000 compounding at 2% for fifty years only grows to $27,000, just 1% of what you were expecting. Even if you attain that 6% return, which is probably optimistic, that $10,000 will only grow into $184,000. To make matters worse, doctors don't begin saving when they're twenty. Age thirty-five would be more realistic. Most physicians don't want to work until age seventy either, more like sixty. So instead of having fifty years, they've got twenty-five. A total of $10,000 invested for twenty-five years compounding at 4% only grows into the depressingly low figure of $27,000 after 2½ decades! The money you invest in your forties and fifties is going to have even less time to compound.

## The Rule of 72

The rule of 72 is a way to determine how quickly your money will grow at any given interest rate. Divide the interest rate into 72, and the result is the number of years it takes your money to double. So if your investment earned 7.2%, your money would double every ten years. At 12%, your money would double every six years. In a savings account paying 1%, your money will take over seven decades to double. Your rate of return really matters, especially over long periods of time.

## Why Your Money Won't Grow At 12% per Year

First, the frequently used 12% figure usually comes from the S&P 500 returns from 1927 to the present, currently about 11.8%. That number is also an average (arithmetic) mean, not an annualized (geometric) mean or CAGR (compound annual growth rate). Basically, you don't get 11.8% a year because when the value of an investment goes down 50%, it has to go up 100% to get back to even. When you account for that drag from the volatility of the investment, you get an annualized return. For the S&P 500, this is about 2% less, currently 9.8%.

Very few investors hold a portfolio consisting entirely of stocks. Usually, they hold some less risky investments, too, such as CDs or bonds, especially as they get older and closer to retirement. Less risky investments generally have lower returns. Given our current historically low interest rates, bonds have an expected return of about 2% right now. Even if you still believe stocks have an expected return of 10% (and many experts do not), a portfolio of 50% stocks and 50% bonds only has an expected return of 6%. Now you need to adjust this for inflation. Over the last 100 years, inflation has averaged about 3%. So now we're down to 3%. We haven't even mentioned investment expenses (that 1% fee you're paying your advisor now seems pretty large doesn't it?) or taxes. It isn't that compound interest doesn't work; it's just that it is extremely difficult to get your money to compound at anywhere near 12% (when adjusted for inflation) for any reasonable length of time. I have tracked my investment returns meticulously over the last decade since I started investing late in my intern year. Despite holding a very aggressive portfolio, paying almost no investment expenses or taxes, my annualized after-inflation portfolio return is still about 6%. If you are planning on after-inflation portfolio returns of 10%–12% over your entire investing career, I can guarantee you will be disappointed, ending up with far less money than you anticipated.

If you are interested in learning how to accurately calculate your own return, I have a blog post on the website that shows how to use the XIRR function in a spreadsheet program like Microsoft Excel to do so. You can find it at http//whitecoatinvestor.com/how-to-calculatc-your-return-the-excel-xirr-function/.

## The Good News about Retirement

I feel really bad about giving you that information. I still recall the disappointment I felt when I realized that just putting a little money away as a young man wasn't going to make me ultra wealthy. However, I'm pleased to be able to give you some very good news as well.

Many people think they need to figure out a way for their investments to replace their entire income in order to retire with the same standard of living that they had prior to retirement. Even financial planners often use a figure of 80% of your income. The truth is that you probably only need your portfolio to replace a very small portion of your peak income as an attending physician in order to have a very comfortable retirement.

Consider all the things you're paying for now that, if you plan properly, you will not be paying in retirement. First, physicians generally pay a large percentage of their income in taxes, often 20%–30% of the gross. This bill will likely be dramatically reduced in retirement. You also won't be paying for retirement savings, a mortgage, work expenses, or expenses for your children. You might have them through college by then. You may even be able to cut back to a single car or downsize into a smaller home with lower property taxes, lower utilities, and lower maintenance costs. You'll drop your life, disability, and malpractice insurance. Many doctors are self-employed and thus pay their own benefits. They may even spend LESS on health care in retirement thanks to Medicare. Those who regularly give a percentage of their income to charity (such as "tithing") will give less to charity due to having less income. When making projections about future income, many people forget to account for Social Security (SS). A physician turning sixty-seven this year who has paid in the maximum SS tax for the last thirty years will receive an inflation-adjusted income of over $30,000 a year from SS. If married to a similar professional, the spouse may get that much again but should at least be getting half of that.

Sure, some expenses will probably go up. You'll have more time to travel and want to spend more on hobbies, and who doesn't like to spoil the grandchildren? But the fact remains that your living expenses will be drastically reduced. Consider the example in Table 7.

| Item | Working Physician | Retired Physician |
|---|---|---|
| Working Income | $300,000 | $0 |
| Portfolio Income | $0 | $46,600 |
| SS Income | $0 | $45,000 |
| Total Income | $300,000 | $91,600 |
|  |  |  |
| Taxes | $75,000 | $12,000 |
| Retirement Savings | $60,000 | $0 |
| Mortgage | $30,000 | $0 |
| College Savings | $15,000 | $0 |
| Work Expenses | $2,000 | $0 |
| Children's Expenses | $15,000 | $0 |
| Life Insurance | $2,000 | $0 |
| Disability Insurance | $3,000 | $0 |
| Health Insurance and Health Care | $7,500 | $10,000 |
| H.S.A. | $6,400 | $0 |
| Charity | $30,000 | $12,500 |
| Transportation | $5,000 | $3,000 |
| Travel | $10,000 | $15,000 |
| Other Expenses | $39,100 | $39,100 |
| Total Expenses | $300,000 | $91,600 |

**Table 7**

This hypothetical physician, who is obviously a pretty good saver, is going to be able to live quite comfortably on less than one-third of his peak income. In fact, once you factor in Social Security, he'll only need his portfolio to provide $46,600 a year, or about 16% of his peak income. Yet, he'll enjoy the same standard of living in retirement as he had prior to retirement. Now everyone is going to be a little bit different. If you run the numbers yourself, you may find you need 25%, 35%, or even 50% of your previous peak income in order to maintain your standard of living. My own personal projections are right around 30%. But the number isn't going to be 80%, much less 100%, especially if you save a reasonable percentage of your income now.

Beware the pitfall of letting your standard of living rise after you pay off your mortgage and get the children through college. If you get used to spending the money freed up by decreased expenses, you'll need a larger retirement portfolio and thus need to work longer to maintain your standard of living in retirement.

## Combining the Good News with the Bad News

A lot of people don't start saving for retirement because they figure it is simply unreachable, especially given the fact that the "magic compounding machine" doesn't work the way they thought it would. Consider a 50-year-old who wants to retire at sixty-seven but really hasn't saved anything at all. He has an income of $300,000, estimates he'll get $45,000 from Social Security, and figures he is going to need $120,000 a year in retirement. He is comfortable with an expected 4% annualized real return from his portfolio. How much does he need to save a year in order to make it? He figures he'll need a nest egg of about $1.875 million in order to provide $75,000 of income from the portfolio each year. To get there in seventeen years at 4% requires that he save $76,000 a year, or about 20%. That's certainly doable and should be good news for those who may be starting a little late. If he had started upon finishing his training at thirty-two, he would have only needed to save about $25,000 a year, or 8% of his peak income. More likely, he would have saved 15% of his income and retired around sixty. Remember that retiring prior to being eligible for Social Security will require you to replace that income as well.

## But Isn't Social Security Going Broke?

Our nation has many fiscal problems, but the easiest one to fix is Social Security. There are a half dozen ways to fix it, and only a little bit of tweaking is required to actually do so. Social Security is one of the most popular programs our government runs, and frankly, works quite well. You might not get quite as much as you anticipate or you might get it a year or two later than you expect or more likely you'll have to pay a little more in Social Security tax during your career, but I think it is highly unlikely that Social Security will disappear completely. If you want to run your projections without it, you're more than welcome to. It will require a higher savings rate and/or more years working. But if you get close to retirement and it looks like Social Security is going to survive after all, then perhaps you can just retire a few years earlier or have a little more luxurious retirement.

You have limited control over your income, your investment returns, and how many years you have to save for retirement, but you have a great deal of control over your savings rate. Set it properly and you'll enjoy the good life both during and after your career.

## Summary of Chapter 7

- Spend a little time with a financial calculator or a spreadsheet when setting your financial goals.
- Save 20% of your income for retirement.
- Expect your money to grow at a rate of just 3%–7% after taxes, expenses, and inflation.
- A typical physician can comfortably retire on just 25%–50% of his preretirement income.

## Recommended Additional Reading

Martin T., Larson P., Larson J. (2012) *Doctor's Eyes Only.* Brockport and Schoolcraft LLC. (Chapter 1: Cash Flow)

http://whitecoatinvestor.com/compound-interest-the-excel-future-value-fv-function/

http://whitecoatinvestor.com/how-to-calculate-your-return-the-excel-xirr-function/

http://whitecoatinvestor.com/percentage-of-current-income-needed-in-retirement/

# Chapter Eight
# The Motorway to Dublin

*"Most investors, both institutional and individual, will find that the best way to own common stocks is through an index fund that charges minimal fees. Those following this path are sure to beat the . . . results [of] the great majority of investment professionals."* — Warren Buffett

Taylor Larimore, one of the authors of *The Bogleheads Guide to Investing*, is fond of saying, "There are many roads to Dublin." He means that there are many different ways you can invest and still arrive at your goal. However, some "roads" are faster and more reliable. The fastest, most reliable roads in the United States are called interstates. In the British Isles, they are called motorways and abbreviated "M1," "M2," etc. In this chapter, I'm going to explain how to get onto the "motorway" and stay on it until you get to your destination of a comfortable retirement. There are many other ways to invest, and it's possible that if you're lucky you may even find a shortcut or two by getting off the motorway from time to time. But you should still learn about the motorway and consider it your "default" investing method. It is a safe and reliable investing strategy for a busy professional.

### Additional Study Required

The Recommended Additional Reading section at the end of this chapter is particularly lengthy and provides further explanation of most of the terms and concepts discussed in this chapter. In order to keep this book short enough so that readers will actually complete it, I will only be able to provide a brief overview of the most important investing concepts for you to understand. This book does not, and cannot, provide comprehensive investing advice. If parts of this chapter seem confusing or overwhelming to you, I encourage you to explore the recommended additional resources, beginning with the easier books at the top of the list.

### The Basics of Investing

At this point, it is worthwhile to review some basic investing definitions. A **stock** is a share of a company, such as Disney or Apple. If Apple sells lots of iPads, the value of the company increases, and it pays out more money as a dividend to its owners, i.e., those who own shares of stock. A **bond** is a loan, either to a company or to a government entity, such as the US Treasury. The treasury pays you interest on that loan every year. After the term of the bond is up, it will pay you back the principal. **Real estate** is a physical property that charges rent to its tenants. A **mutual fund** is a group of investors who pool their money together to buy dozens or hundreds of different stocks, bonds, or properties in order to provide diversification. Some mutual funds are "actively managed" and try to predict which stocks and bonds (collectively, securities) are going to do well in the future. Other mutual funds are "passively managed" and simply try to capture the return of the market by buying all the securities. These passively managed "index funds" own both winners and losers but do so at such a low cost that they outperform the average actively managed fund, especially over the long run. Many studies demonstrate that it is very difficult for an active mutual fund manager to outperform an index fund by more than the additional expenses incurred by the active management.

There are lots of things in investing that cannot be controlled. You cannot control the political situation in the world. You cannot control the actions of the Federal Reserve on short-term interest rates, and even the Fed cannot control long-term interest rates. You cannot control which companies, municipalities, or even countries will default on their debt. You cannot control which companies or industries will do well and which will do poorly. You cannot predict the future. You need an investment plan that doesn't require you to do so. Focusing your investment efforts on five factors that are within your control—risk, diversification, investment expenses, taxes, and your own behavior—will keep you on the Motorway to Dublin.

### The Five Investing Factors within Your Control

### 1. Risk

Risk is a complex subject, and volumes have been written on it. One of the first risks that most investors are exposed to is market risk, i.e., the risk that they will lose money that they invest in the market. These are really two risks lumped into one.

The first is the risk that your investment will go down in value and not come back for a while. This is basically volatility and is relatively easily overcome. First, do not put money into the market that you need anytime soon and second, do not look at the market when it is doing poorly or simply take a lot of antacids so you can sleep at night during bear markets. The reason you cannot sleep at night is really due to the second risk, and that is the fact that sometimes the value of your investment does not come back at all. This "deep risk" (a coin termed by William Bernstein in his recent book of the same title) is actually a much greater risk than just volatility (a shallow risk), which a patient investor can just wait out. It is also the reason that high-volatility investments cause many investors to shoot themselves in the foot by buying high and selling low. They fear that this time the markets might not come back.

There are other risks out there, including individual security risk, sector risk, manager risk, credit risk, default risk, and interest rate risk. However, after market risk, the most important risk to keep in mind is the risk of not meeting your investment goals.

Unfortunately, two significant factors are working against you in the race to acquire a decent nest egg. The first is that you have limited time, especially if you had a late start on saving for retirement. The second is inflation. While no one likes investment volatility or running the risk that their money will disappear forever, it is important to be sure you are taking enough risk to ensure your returns outpace inflation. This is the reason most experts advise you to include risky assets in your portfolio. Safer assets, such as bonds, are likely to have a return ranging from just below to just above the inflation rate. So you want to take enough risk to meet your goals, but no more, and you want to be sure you are only taking risks for which you are compensated.

## 2. Diversification

The simplest way to decrease risk is to avoid putting all your eggs into one basket (diversification). You want to spread your money out not only between different asset classes (such as stocks, bonds, and real estate) but also within those asset classes. You are not compensated for taking individual security risk, so you should buy dozens or even hundreds of individual securities in each asset class. This can be done easily for most asset classes using mutual funds or exchange traded funds (ETFs-mutual funds traded on stock exchanges.)

## 3. Investing Expenses

One of the biggest contributions made by Jack Bogle, founder of Vanguard, was to point out that, in investing, you get what you DON'T pay for. He refers to the "tyranny of compounding costs" in describing the effects of high investment expenses on the growth of your portfolio.

If two investors make the same 8% per year before expenses on a lump sum investment and the first is paying 2% per year in investment expenses and the second is paying 0.1% per year, then after thirty years the second investor will have 70% more money than the first.

Costs matter, and they matter a lot. Over the long term, index funds outperform the vast majority of actively managed mutual funds primarily because their costs are so much lower but also because they do not run manager risk, the risk that the expert choosing which securities to buy and which to sell will guess wrong. Numerous studies show that very few actively managed mutual fund managers can outperform an index fund when expenses are taken into account, and those few who will outperform cannot be identified in advance.

## 4. Tax Efficiency

Investing is a constant battle against inflation, investment expenses, and taxes. Physicians tend to be in the highest tax brackets, and taxes are frequently their most significant investment expense. Taxes should not be an overriding consideration in how you invest, but taxes will reduce your investment returns every year,and investing in a tax-efficient manner can cut years off the time required to become financially independent.

Perhaps the best way to minimize investment-related taxation is through the use of retirement accounts. Think of a retirement account as a piece of luggage, such as a backpack or suitcase. They are all used to carry clothing but are useful in different situations. In this analogy, investments like stocks, bonds, and mutual funds become the clothes. Any piece of clothing can go into any piece of luggage.

Retirement accounts include employer provided tax-deferred retirement investing accounts, such as 401(k)s, 403(b)s, 457(b)s, and Defined Benefit Plans. They also include nonemployer provided retirement investment accounts, such as traditional and Roth Individual Retirement Arrangements (IRAs) and self-employed retirement investment accounts, such as Individual 401(k)s, Simplified Employee Pension IRAs (SEP-IRAs), and Savings Incentive Match PLan for Employees (SIMPLE IRAs). These accounts avoid the drag that taxes place on a taxable investing account that is taxed each year on its distributed dividends and capital gains. Tax-deferred investing accounts such as 401(k)s also provide an arbitrage between the higher marginal tax rate at which you contribute funds in your peak earning years and the lower effective tax rate at which you withdraw funds in retirement. Roth 401(k)s and Roth IRAs are post-tax investing accounts named after Senator William Roth. They do not provide a tax arbitrage, but money contributed to the account is never subject to income taxes again. In general, an employed physician will have access to a 401(k), an academic physician will be provided a 403(b) and perhaps a 457(b), a partner physician will have a 401(k)/profit-sharing plan (allowing larger contributions than a typical 401(k)), and an independent contractor should use an Individual 401(k). We'll also discuss three other accounts that physicians need to know about, including the Backdoor Roth IRA, the Stealth IRA, and the taxable investing account.

Most physicians should be taking advantage of a loophole placed into the tax code in 2010 that I like to call the **Backdoor Roth** IRA. Prior to 2010, there was an income limit on who could contribute directly to a Roth IRA or convert a traditional IRA to a Roth IRA. In 2014, that limit ranges from a modified adjusted gross income of $114,000 (single) to a $191,000 (married), disqualifying most physicians. However, beginning in 2010, that income limit was eliminated for conversions (but not direct contributions). What does that mean? That means a high-income physician can contribute to a nondeductible traditional IRA and then immediately convert it to a Roth IRA, essentially funding a Roth IRA "through the back door."

Remember that if you have a retirement plan at work and your income is over $70,000 ($116,000 married) you cannot deduct traditional IRA contributions. You can still make them, though, thus the "nondeductible" traditional IRA.

There is a catch to the backdoor Roth IRA in that the physician must ensure he has no money in any type of IRA, including self-employed retirement accounts, such as SEP-IRAs or SIMPLE IRAs, at the end of that calendar year to prevent a "pro-rata calculation" that nullifies most of the benefit of the conversion. To avoid this complication, the investor typically will either roll IRA money into a 401(k) or just convert the entire IRA to a Roth IRA. The same procedure can also be followed for a spousal Roth IRA to allow another $5,500 ($6,500 if fifty or older) to be saved for retirement. Your spouse does not have to have any earned income for you to contribute to his or her spousal IRA. A how-to guide for the backdoor Roth IRA can be found at here://whitecoatinvestor.com/backdoor-roth-ira-tutorial/.

Many physicians should also be using a Health Savings Account (HSA), which I like to refer to as a **"Stealth IRA."** If you use a qualified high-deductible health insurance plan (and most physicians should), in 2014 you are allowed to contribute up to $3,300 (single) or $6,500 (family) to an HSA. That money is deducted from your taxes. HSA money can be invested in just about anything, just like a typical retirement account. The money grows in a tax-protected manner, and as long as it is spent on health care, is not taxed upon withdrawal either. Fidelity Investments suggests that couples retiring in 2013 will need $220,000 just to cover health care costs in retirement. A HSA is a great way to save up that money.

If, in retirement, you decide to spend your HSA money on a boat, there is no penalty, but you do have to pay taxes on the money just like any other tax-deferred retirement account. However, there is a significant loophole you should be aware of.

If you keep a record and receipts for approved health expenditures you made over the years, you can avoid paying taxes on money you withdraw in retirement and then spend on items other than health care. At the current time, there is no rule saying you must pull the money out of the HSA in the same year you incur the approved health expenditure. It would not surprise me to see this loophole changed in the future, but for now, it is easy enough to keep a running list of your HSA-eligible health care expenditures.

There are other health care–related savings accounts, such as a flexible spending account (FSA) or a Health Reimbursement Account (HRA) that may be offered by your employer. I encourage you to use these "use it or lose it" type accounts to reduce your taxes, but they cannot hold money in the account year to year as an HSA can. You can learn more about using a HSA as a Stealth IRA at here://whitecoatinvestor.com/retirement-accounts/the-stealth-ira/.

Many physicians will also end up having to use a **taxable investing account** simply because they need to save more money than will fit into their retirement accounts, even if they include a personal and spousal backdoor Roth IRA and an HSA. Although a standard brokerage or mutual fund account suffers from tax drag and doesn't have the same asset protection and estate planning benefits as a retirement account, it can still be highly tax efficient.

The key is to only place very tax-efficient investments into it, such as low-turnover broadly diversified stock index funds and municipal bond funds. The wise investor will also take advantage of lower long-term capital gains tax rates, qualified dividend tax rates, tax-loss harvesting opportunities, charitable donations, and the step-up in basis at death. In fact, for an aggressive tax-loss harvester who makes large charitable donations each year, it is possible for a taxable investing account to actually LOWER your tax bill each year. More information on using a taxable investing account in a tax-efficient manner can be found at http://whitecoatinvestor.com/retirement-accounts/ the-taxable-investment-account-2/.

Many investors struggle with the decision of whether or not to contribute to a tax-deferred account, such as a 401(k), or to a tax-free account, such as a Roth IRA. This is a complicated decision, but there are a few rules of thumb to follow.

First, when only one is available, you might as well contribute to it. For example, if your employer offers a traditional tax-deferred 401(k) but doesn't offer a Roth 401(k), you might as well use the tax-deferred option. Likewise, most physicians are not eligible to make deductible traditional IRA contributions, so they might as well make Roth IRA contributions, either directly or "through the backdoor."

Second, physicians in relatively low tax brackets, such as residents and military doctors, should preferentially use Roth accounts. Likewise, physicians in their peak earning years should preferentially use tax-deferred accounts.

In retirement, it is ideal to have some of your money in tax-deferred accounts and some in Roth accounts. By withdrawing from both, you can "fill up" the lower tax brackets with the as-yet-untaxed tax-deferred account withdrawals and then take the rest of your spending from the Roth accounts, minimizing your taxes in retirement. Also keep in mind that you must begin withdrawing money from tax-deferred accounts at age 70 ½. These required minimum distributions (RMD) do not apply to Roth accounts. More information on choosing between Roth 401(k) and traditional 401(k) contributions can be found at http://whitecoatinvestor.com/should-you-make-roth-or-traditional-401k-contributions/.

## 5. Behavior

Inflation, expenses, and taxes are worthy adversaries to the typical investor, but perhaps his biggest enemy stares back at him from the mirror each morning. Studies show that investors make the same errors over and over again. Investors are notorious for investing with their emotions and chasing performance by repeatedly buying high and selling low. Jason Zweig, in his groundbreaking book *Your Money and Your Brain*, said, "Your investing brain does not just add and multiply and estimate and evaluate. When you win, lose, or risk money, you stir up some of the most profound emotions a human being can ever feel."

Investors frequently fall victim to herd behavior (following the crowd), loss aversion (losses hurt more than gains help), mental accounting (ignoring the overall portfolio and focusing on just one part), recency bias (projecting the recent past into the future), and paralysis by analysis (not doing anything because there are too many choices). However, the most disastrous behavioral error that investors make is to sell long-term investments at low prices in response to short-term events. While financial education, experience, and a well-designed written investment plan help, do not overestimate your ability to stay the course in turbulent markets. It is better to have a less-aggressive plan with lower expected returns than to have a plan that will self-destruct due to your inability to control your own behavior. As with the game show *The Price Is Right,* you want to get as close to your maximal risk tolerance as possible without going over.

### Fixed Asset Allocation of Index Funds

So what is the "Motorway to Dublin" really? It is a plan that focuses on the factors you can control—avoiding unnecessary risks, diversification, investment costs, taxes, and your own behavior. It is a plan that does not require you to predict the future to be successful. It is an annually rebalanced, fixed asset allocation of three to ten asset classes invested in low-cost index funds. For example, you might decide on an asset allocation that is 40% US Stocks, 20% International Stocks, and 40% Bonds. You can find 150 other reasonable investing portfolios that will get you onto the "Motorway to Dublin" here:http://whitecoatinvestor.com/150-portfolios-better-than-yours/.

You implement your plan by purchasing the lowest-cost index funds invested in these asset classes that are available to you. Then, if stocks do poorly that year and bonds do well, you direct your new contributions to the stock asset classes and if necessary even sell some of the bonds to buy more stocks. At the end of the year, your balance is higher, but you still have the same asset allocation. A reasonably diversified asset allocation helps your nest egg to outpace inflation without taking on unnecessary risk. Retirement accounts and low-turnover index funds minimize your tax bill and investment costs. The fixed asset allocation ensures you are constantly buying low, avoiding the need to predict the future to be successful, and allows you to avoid the behavioral errors likely to torpedo the best designed investment plan. In times of market turmoil, you merely need to refer to your written investment plan and follow it. You can go for literally months without looking at your investments or investment-related news.

**Steps For Designing and Implementing Your Portfolio**

1.  Choose your goals and determine how much you will need to save for each of them
2.  Choose which types of accounts you will use to save and in what proportion
3.  Determine an asset allocation likely to meet your goals
4.  Select low cost investments to fulfill your asset allocation
5.  Rebalance your portfolio back to your original allocation once a year

There are certainly other ways to invest, just as there are many roads to Dublin. The vast majority, but not quite all of my money is invested in index funds. Many physicians have had success buying rental properties in their hometown or even joining with other investors and purchasing rental property all over the country. You may also be presented with opportunities to invest in imaging centers, urgent cares, or surgical centers. Each of these opportunities should be evaluated carefully on its own merits and may offer high returns, tax advantages, asset protection benefits, and diversification for your index fund portfolio. Do yourself a favor, though, by making sure you have a very good reason anytime you deviate from this default "Motorway to Dublin" investment strategy. You certainly do not have to buy real estate, small businesses, or cash value life insurance in order to reach financial independence. You can easily and reliably reach your goals by doing nothing but practicing good medicine, saving 20% of your income, and buying and holding an index mutual fund portfolio.

**Summary of Chapter 8**

- A good portfolio is broadly diversified, low cost, mostly or completely passively managed, and appropriately risky.
- The amount of risk you should take depends on your unique ability, need, and desire to take risk.
- Market risk is less important than the risk of not meeting your goals, but do not overestimate your ability to tolerate investment losses.
- Managing your behavior matters more than optimizing your asset allocation.
- Most physicians should be using a personal and spousal Backdoor Roth IRA.
- A Health Savings Account (HSA) is an excellent supplemental retirement fund.
- You can be financially successful without investing in anything but a handful of index funds.

**Recommended Additional Reading**

This chapter, in particular, was only able to skim the surface of the investment knowledge a do-it-yourself investor will need to acquire in order to be successful. As such, unless you'll be hiring a good investment manager, try to read a good investing book at least once a year. The books below are listed from easiest to hardest to digest.

Van Ness, R. (2011) *Common Sense Investing.* Self-published using CreateSpace.

Schultheis, B. (2009) *The New Coffeehouse Investor.* New York, NY: The Penguin Group.

Roth, A.S. (2009) *How a Second Grader Beats Wall Street.* Hoboken, NJ: John Wiley & Sons, Inc.

Tobias, A. (2005) *The Only Investment Guide You'll Ever Need.* Orlando, FL: Harcourt Books.

Larimore, T., Lindauer, M., Leboeuf, M. (2006) T*he Bogleheads Guide To Investing.* Hoboken, NJ: John Wiley & Sons, Inc.

Zweig, J. (2007) *Your Money And Your Brain.* New York, NY: Simon and Schuster.

Bernstein, W. J. (2010) *The Investor's Manifesto.* Hoboken, NJ: John Wiley & Sons, Inc.

Ferri, R.A. (2006) *All About Asset Allocation.* New York, NY: The McGraw-Hill Companies, Inc.

Bogle, J.C. (1999) *Common Sense on Mutual Funds.* New York, NY: John Wiley & Sons, Inc.

Swedroe, L.E. (2011) *The Quest for Alpha.* Hoboken, NJ: John Wiley & Sons, Inc.

http://www.bogleheads.org/wiki/main_page

http://whitecoatinvestor.com/retirement-accounts/backdoor-roth-ira/

http://whitecoatinvestor.com/retirement-accounts/the-stealth-ira/

http://whitecoatinvestor.com/retirement-accounts/the-taxable-investment-accounts-2/

http://whitecoatinvestor.com/cash-balance-plans-another-retirement-plan-for-professionals/

http://whitecoatinvestor.com/active-mutual-fund-managers-not-getting-any-betetr/

http://whitecoatinvestor.com/designing-your-portfolio-part-1-goal-setting/

http://whitecoatinvestor.com/150-portfolios-better-than-yours/

# Chapter Nine
# Getting Off the Motorway

*"Never count on making a good sale. Have the purchase price be so attractive that even a mediocre sale gives good results."* — Warren Buffett

In the last chapter, I discussed the "default" investing strategy that you should use, namely a diversified, fixed asset allocation of low-cost index mutual funds. In this chapter, I will make a few comments about some of the common side roads you will be tempted to take en route to investment bliss.

## Real Estate Investing

Real estate is a viable way to reach investing success. Many physicians invest in real estate as part, or even all, of their portfolio. A surprising number have left medicine completely to work in real estate full-time. One of the greatest benefits of investing in real estate is that it is generally safer to leverage income-producing real estate when compared with other investments, such as mutual funds. Investors typically buy a property with just a 20%–50% down payment, yet they control the cash flow, appreciation, and tax benefits for the entire investment.

## How Real Estate Investments Make Money

You make money in real estate in four different ways: appreciation, tax breaks, amortization, and cash flow.

**Appreciation** is the easiest to understand. If you buy the property at one pnice then sell it at a higher price, you get to keep the difference. If you were highly leveraged by using a small down payment, your return from appreciation may be quite high. If you put $40,000 down on a $200,000 house and it appreciates to $300,000 over five years, your return would be 28% per year! Of course, if the house dropped in value just 20% from $200,000 to $160,000, your entire investment would be wiped out for a 100% loss.

Real estate investing benefits from many different **tax breaks**. Perhaps the largest is depreciation. Your rental property is a business like any other. Equipment and buildings wear out, so the government allows you to depreciate them each year on your taxes. Residential rental property is depreciated over 27.5 years, so you multiply your basis in the property (basically the value you bought it for) by 3.6% and subtract that from your income on the property each year. This allows a portion of your income to be tax free. Many real estate investors can actually make money on real estate overall but claim a loss on their taxes thanks to depreciation. High-income professionals, such as physicians, however, are not able to use passive losses to lower their taxable income from their main job. Upon selling a property, depreciation is "recaptured" and must be paid but only at 25%. If your marginal tax rate is 33%, then saving taxes at 33% and paying them at 25% is a good deal.

**Amortization** is money that is used to pay down your loan. You might not have any extra money in your pocket at the end of the year, but the loan you took out to purchase the property has been paid down a few thousand dollars. That's part of your investment return.

**Cash flow** is perhaps the most important way that an investment property generates a return for you. If you purchase a property for $200,000 without a loan and the rent on this property is $1,500 per month, then the gross rent is $18,000 per year. There is a rule of thumb called **The 55% Rule** which helps you determine your **net operating income** by multiplying your gross rents by 55%. This is because about 45% of gross rents will go toward such expenses as maintenance, management fees, taxes, insurance, and vacancies. Multiplying $18,000 by 55% leaves you with a net operating income of

$9,900. Your capitalization rate on this property is $9,900/$200,000, or about 5%. **Capitalization rate** is one way that investors compare one property with another. A capitalization rate of 10% is quite good, and a capitalization rate of 3% is relatively poor. A low capitalization rate doesn't necessarily mean the investment will have poor overall returns, since cash flow is only one aspect of the return from real estate investment, but all else being equal a higher capitalization rate is better.

### Real Estate Is a Second Job

The worst part about real estate investing is that it is a combination of an investment and a second job. The default investing method discussed in the last chapter requires little time, expertise, or effort. Successful real estate investing requires all of these. It is difficult to be both an expert in your medical specialty and an expert in an entirely different field, such as real estate. Physicians get enough calls at 3 a.m. from the hospital; they don't need any from their tenants. Acquiring, maintaining, and managing rental property requires time, which is a precious commodity for a busy professional. You can choose to do as much of the labor in real estate yourself as you like and pay someone else to do what you do not like. Many private real estate investments (as well as investing in a type of stock called REITs) require nothing more than a check from you. Keep in mind that every fee you pay is subtracted directly from your investment return.

However, if you are interested in a part-time job that may prove to be very lucrative, real estate is a great one to choose. Unlike the stock market, the real estate market is very inefficient and even more irrational. Skill and intelligence are rewarded, and the lack of skill may be severely punished, especially when compounded by the effects of leverage.

### Looking At Your Home as an Investment

Many people have been conditioned by realtors to view a home as a great investment. In some ways, this is true. The "dividend" from owning your own home is that you don't have to pay rent to live somewhere else. However, you will be better served by considering your home a consumption item. Buying a home that is too expensive will erode your financial security. It can cost a great deal of money to heat, cool, insure, maintain, repair, buy, and sell a home. When purchasing a home, you would do well to consider it from an investment point of view. Most homes are priced based on what other homes like them have sold for in the recent past with little consideration of what it would cost to rent a similar home. I suggest that prior to purchase you evaluate the home from the point of view of an investor. If you can rent a similar home for $2,000 but you have to spend $600,000 to purchase it, that means it has a cap rate of only = $2,000 X 12 months X 55% / $600,000 = 2.2%. You are almost surely better off renting that home than purchasing it. On the other hand, if the home will sell for $400,000 and rents for $4,000, then your cap rate is 6.6%, which is quite good.

## Some Guidelines for Home Purchasing

Some physicians have no idea how much they can or should spend on a home. I will give two guidelines that I think will serve physicians well. The first is to never carry a mortgage larger than twice your gross income. The second is to spend less than 20% of your gross income on housing, including your mortgage payment, utilities, property taxes, insurance, and maintenance.

You can be assured that lenders will lend you much more than this amount. Just because a lender says you can afford to take on more debt doesn't mean you actually can. Spending more than this will require you to make sacrifices in your other lifestyle choices, including the ability to choose when you will retire and how much you will live on in retirement. Physicians in high cost of living areas, such as California or Manhattan, will quickly see that it is difficult or impossible to acquire high-quality housing for that price in their locale. They may find they have to spend three or even four times their gross income for a house. It is acceptable to do so but realize it will require significant sacrifice in other areas of your financial life to own such an expensive home. However, a physician making $200,000 per year should not be shopping for a $1 million home much less a $2 million home.

Many banks will offer you a "physician mortgage." These specialized products charge you higher interest rates and/or fees in return for allowing you to put down less than 20% on a home purchase without paying Private Mortgage Insurance (PMI). PMI has no benefit to you. It is simply insurance to protect your lender from you defaulting on your payments. As a general rule, I recommend against physician mortgages. In my view, if you do not have a 20% down payment or cannot afford to pay for the house on a 15-year fixed mortgage, you can't afford the house. That said, a physician just out of training may have much better uses for his cash (such as paying down high-interest rate student loans or funding retirement accounts) than using it to get a better deal on a mortgage. As discussed in chapter six, if you live like a resident for a couple of years after residency, you should have enough cash to pay down student loans, maximize retirement account contributions, and still come up with a 20% down payment on a reasonable house.

### Don't Mix Insurance and Investing

Nearly every physician will receive a pitch for whole life insurance, universal life insurance, variable life insurance, or an annuity at some point in his life. As a general rule, mixing insurance and investing is not a good idea.

You do not need any of these products to be financially successful. These are complex products, and the more complex the better for the insurance company and the agent, and the worse for you. These are products that are sold, not bought. For this reason, the commissions offered to agents to sell them can be very high.

For example, an agent who sells you a whole life insurance policy with a premium of $40,000 per year will typically receive a commission between $20,000 and $44,000 for the sale. As you might imagine, that commission can be highly motivating, especially since the median income for insurance agents is just $47,000 per year. To make matters worse, many of the worst policies offer the highest commissions. As a result of this ridiculous conflict of interest, agents often throw out some serious myths in an effort to persuade you to buy their product. This probably explains the rather damning statistic that 80% or more of those who buy this product get rid of it prior to death. Perhaps that is why personal finance guru Dave Ramsey calls whole life insurance the "Pay Day Loan of The Middle Class."

**Whole life insurance** can be set up in many different ways, but in general you pay a monthly or annual premium for either a defined period of time or until you die. The longer the period of time over which you pay the premiums, the lower the premiums will be. Whenever you die, your beneficiary gets the proceeds of the policy. Since every whole life policy is guaranteed to pay out if you just hold onto it to your death, the premiums are much higher than a comparable term life insurance policy. A whole life insurance policy, like other types of permanent life insurance, is really a hybrid of insurance and investment.

That cash value grows in a tax-protected manner, and you can even borrow money from the policy tax free (but not interest free). Upon your death, whatever you borrowed (plus the interest) is taken out of the death benefit, and the rest is paid to your beneficiary. You get the cash value or the death benefit, not both. This investment aspect allows those who sell this product to find all kinds of creative reasons why you should buy it and creative ways to structure it. The most extreme advocates may even argue that you do not need ANY other financial products during your entire life since whole life insurance can apparently take care of all your needs, including mortgages, consumer loans, insurance, investments, college savings, and retirement. The problem is that for every use of whole life insurance, there is usually a better way to deal with that financial issue. Investors will generally find they will be much better off covering their life insurance needs with an inexpensive term policy and investing the difference into a portfolio of index funds.

Further discussion of whole life insurance and other hybrid insurance/investment products is beyond the scope of this book, but you can learn more at: http//whitecoatinvestor.com/debunking-the-myths-of-whole-lofe-insurance/.


### Private Investments

Most physicians will be approached at some point with an opportunity to invest in a private investment of some type. It may be a real estate deal, a surgical center, an urgent care, an imaging center, or perhaps some other type of business. Each of these needs to be weighed on an individual basis. Some may be wonderful investments, but many will not be.

Remember that physicians, like successful artists and professional athletes, make their living by having a skill that results in a high income despite not having a high degree of business skill. As with real estate investing, there is potential for significant profit in private investments, but it is hardly an efficient market. Some investors will do very well, and some will make out poorly. Make sure you understand the risks and can afford the worst-case scenario before leaving the Motorway to Dublin for these opportunities. If you are not going to take the time to do the due diligence required, stick with an index fund portfolio. As Warren Buffet likes to say, in investing there are no "called strikes." It's okay not to swing at every investment that crosses the plate. You can stand there all day watching pitches go by until you see one you understand and are confident will be a good deal.

## Other Investments

There are many investments out there that I haven't discussed in this book, including precious metals, commodities, peer to peer lending, hedge funds, private equity funds, junk bonds, bitcoins, art, baseball cards, options, currencies, convertible bonds, covered calls, and preferred stock among others. You do not need to invest in any of these to be successful. Investing can be very simple. If you do decide to dabble in these more exotic investments, limit your investment to a small portion of your portfolio, perhaps no more than 5%–10%, and keep the vast majority of your portfolio in boring old stocks, bonds, and real estate. In investing, like baseball, hitting singles and avoiding errors is a better strategy than swinging for the fences. You don't want an investment plan that requires you to be able to predict the future to be successful.

**Summary of Chapter 9**

- Real estate investing can be a great way to boost returns and diversify your portfolio.
- Good real estate investing requires much more work than investing in index funds.
- Don't overpay for your house. Limit your mortgage to twice your gross salary.
- Don't mix insurance and investing. You don't need to purchase cash value life insurance or annuities to achieve financial success, and most people who purchase them end up regretting their decision.
- Private investments can be a great deal, but each must be evaluated individually. Due diligence is key.

**Recommended Additional Reading**

Swedroe, L.E., and Kizer, J. (2008) *The Only Guide to Alternative Investments You'll Ever Need.* New York, NY: Bloomberg Press.

Reed, J.T. (2009) *Best Practices for the Intelligent Real Estate Investor.* Alamo, CA: John T. Reed.

Gallinelli, F. (2008) *What Every Real Estate Investor Needs To Know About Cash Flow.* New York, NY: The McGraw-Hill Companies, Inc.

http://whitecatinvestor.com/debunking the myths of whole life insurance/

http://whitecatinvestor.com/4-ways-to-add-real-estate-to-your-portfolio/

http://whitecatinvestor.com/real-estate-private-placements-series-part-5-of-5/

# Chapter Ten
# Paying the Help

*"We do not all need to hire a full-time driver if we only need directions"*
— Tom Nowak, CFP

"The help" is usually a somewhat derogatory term referring to household servants. In this chapter, I'd like to talk about a different kind of help, specifically that of insurance agents, financial planners, asset managers, accountants, and attorneys. Let me first get a few caveats out of the way. Most physicians will hire a financial advisor and/or an asset manager to help them make financial decisions and manage their portfolio. I do not have a problem with physicians paying a fair price for good advice. Unfortunately, the vast majority of those who bill themselves as financial advisors neither charge a fair price nor give good advice. More than any other market I know, the market for financial advice is *Caveat Emptor*, Latin for "let the buyer beware."

## What Does It Take To Become a Financial Planner

It turns out that very few people want to have a long-term relationship with someone who calls himself a mutual fund salesman, a stockbroker, or an insurance salesman. So, instead, those who are in these lines of work call themselves "financial advisors," "wealth managers," "financial consultants," or "financial planners." The barriers to giving financial advice professionally are disturbingly low, often requiring little more than a week's worth of education and a multiple choice exam. A quick Internet search for job openings for these folks will reveal the typical requirements (this is a direct quote from an ad seeking advisors for a well-known firm):

- Results-driven, highly motivated, self-starter who possesses integrity, a strong work ethic and the desire to help others plan for and protect their financial futures.
- Team player who possesses excellent interpersonal skills and communication abilities, with a high degree of self-confidence.
- Ability to draw upon past/present experiences and a cquaintances to develop markets and build upon them to sustain long-term relationships.
- Must be a US Citizen or permanent resident.
- A four-year college degree is preferred and relevant professional FINRA securities registrations are a plus.
- If you do not have the following, you will be required to attain them, under [our] sponsorship: state(s) life and health licenses, FINRA Series 7 and 66 registrations.
- MBA, JD, CFP®, CPA or ChFC a plus.

Let me summarize. You have to want the job; you have to be willing to hit up your family, friends, and acquaintances to buy insurance and investments through the firm; and you must be a US citizen or permanent resident. No college degree required. No registrations or licenses required. No advanced degree or time-consuming certifications required.

If experience is required or desired, it is experience in SALES that is relevant, not experience investing or providing advice. Let there be no doubt in your mind that the vast majority of those billing themselves as financial advisors are simply salesmen with little financial training whose goal is to transfer as much of your portfolio into their pockets as possible. They might describe themselves as experts with money, just as you're an expert on hearts, or colons, or on the health of children. But if a physician requires eight years of school and 10,000–20,000 hours of training, is it really fair to compare him to an advisor who studied 40 hours for a couple of tests and went to some company-sponsored sales presentations? Of course not.

## Costs Matter

William Bernstein, MD, in his excellent book *The Four Pillars of Investing*, stated that when you invest,

*"you will be forced to confront the colossus that bestrides the modern American scene: the financial industry. And make no mistake about it, you are engaged in a brutal zero-sum contest with it—every penny of commissions, fees, and transactional costs it extracts is irretrievably lost to you."*

I recently had a discussion with a colleague about the fees he is paying in his 401(k). In this particular 401(k), his first expense is a mutual fund expense ratio in the 0.5%–1.0% range. Second, the 401(k) charges a fee of 0.4% of every dollar in the plan. Finally, he pays a financial advisor 1% a year to decide which of the funds to invest in and to do the actual task of investing the money and rebalancing it. The total fees he is paying add up to over 2% a year. Those fees come directly from his investment return. Consider that he may make 8% a year on his investments, before fees. If he is paying 2% in fees, that is the equivalent of earning 6% a year. Sure, 2% might not seem like much, but if you invest $50,000 a year for thirty years, that little 2% will make a difference of nearly $2 million ($6.1M versus $4.2M). The truth is that 2% isn't rare at all. In fact, it might even be less than average.

You cannot invest for free. There are always some expenses involved. But you can pay far less than 2% a year if you just take a moment to shop around. In my 401(k), I pay mutual fund expense ratios averaging about 0.10%, about 0.10% in 401(k) expenses, and no advisory fees. That's about one-tenth of what my colleague is paying. That is a guaranteed boost to my returns of 1.8% a year, which may be worth over $2 million thirty years from now. In investing, unlike many other areas of life, you literally GET (to keep) what you DON'T pay for. Even if you are getting very good advice and service, it is to your benefit to pay as little as possible for it. Doing as many financial tasks as possible on your own may be very profitable to you over the years. If nothing else, at least find out what fees you're already paying. These fees can be found in your 401(k) plan document, on a website like heep//morningstar.com that lists the expenses of your mutual funds, or on the website of your financial advisor. If you cannot easily discover the fees you are paying, that likely means they are far too high, and time spent looking for them may be highly rewarding.

## Getting Good Advice Can Be Difficult

To make matters worse, the vast majority of "financial advisors" not only charge too much, but they also give poor advice. This is partially a result of lack of education and training. It isn't that they are not trained; the problem is that their training is in sales. But you cannot expect someone with little investing experience and little investing education to actually know much.

A bigger problem is that the "advisor" has serious conflicts of interest. Stockbrokers, mutual fund salesmen, realtors, and insurance salesmen are paid a percentage of the commissions they generate. A stockbroker's incentive, therefore, is to generate as many fees and commissions as possible. Instead of having his goals aligned with yours, he is incentivized to do exactly the opposite of what you need.

A mutual fund salesman gets paid a commission, or a load, when you buy or sell a mutual fund. The load may be as much as 8%. So if you invest $1,000 with him, $80 goes into his pocket and $920 goes into the investment. He doesn't get paid again until he talks you into selling an investment and buying another one. That type of "front-load" is often sold as part of a mutual fund "A" share. Sometimes, the load is a little sneakier. A "B" share has a "back-load," where you pay a commission when you sell instead of when you buy. A "C" share just has the load added to the fund's expense ratio, so you pay it a little bit each year. But whether you buy an A share, a B share, or a C share, the salesman is still getting paid, and a chunk of your money is going into his pocket instead of your investment.

The "advisor" will explain this by saying that this is the way he gets paid for the advice he's providing you. His children need to eat, too, you know. The problem is that not only does this change his incentive to get you to change investments as often as possible, but also loaded mutual funds, especially those with high loads, do not tend to be very good investments. Think about it for a minute. If you had a lousy product to sell, how would you talk salesmen into selling it? By offering them a high commission. As a general rule, the higher the commission, the worse the product. Good products practically sell themselves and don't need to pay a salesman much to sell them. So the worse the mutual fund, the more the salesman makes. Is that the incentive you want your "financial advisor" to have? Of course not.

What these salesmen don't tell you, of course, is that you don't have to pay a load at all. The best mutual funds are sold as "no-load" funds through such companies as Vanguard, DFA, Bridgeway, Fidelity, and T. Rowe Price. But if they talked you into buying those funds, they would not get paid, or at least wouldn't get paid nearly as well.

Realtors are paid based on a percentage of the value of the home you buy. They are incentivized to encourage you to buy the most expensive house you can buy, to pay as much as possible for it, to do so as quickly as possible, and to repeat the process as often as possible. To make matters worse, both the seller's agent and the buyer's agent are paid by the seller. Is this really the person you want giving you advice on buying a home and negotiating on your behalf?

Insurance salesman (also known as agents, brokers, advisors, wealth managers, etc.) have similar conflicts of interest. Cash value life insurance policies and annuities must be sold by licensed agents. Insurance companies pay the agents a commission when they sell a policy. This commission is often 50%–110% of the premiums from the first year of the policy and may also be a small percentage of the premiums paid for the next ten years. Which policies do you suppose offer the best commissions? The worst ones, of course. The agent is incentivized to sell you the largest policy with the largest commission and to do it as often as possible. It isn't that the agent is necessarily a bad person; it's just that the conflicts of interest are difficult for even a good person to overcome.

Some insurance salesmen, as well as mutual fund salesmen, are captive, meaning they can only sell products from a single company. What are the odds that the products of the one company he can sell from are the best ones for you? Not very good. The other serious conflict of interest an insurance salesman has when giving you advice is that he is incentivized to sell you insurance, even if you don't need it, don't want it, or shouldn't buy it. He doesn't get paid if you decide to invest in mutual funds instead nor does he get paid if you decide to take that money and pay down your student loans or mortgage. How can he possibly give you unbiased advice if he gets paid for one option but not the others? He can't, and that's why you shouldn't go to him for advice.

## Figure Out How Your Advisor Gets Paid

The most important thing to learn when choosing an advisor is to figure out how he gets paid. Obviously, you don't want a commissioned salesman as a financial advisor. You want what is referred to as a "fee-only" advisor. Keep in mind that "fee-only" is different from "fee-based." Fee-based advisors charge a fee AND commissions. Even among fee-only advisors there are different ways to get paid. Some charge an hourly fee. Others charge an annual retainer fee. Still others charge you a percentage of your "assets under management" (AUM). Any given advisor may use a combination of these four methods (commissions, hourly, annual retainer, AUM fee) to get paid. Understanding how your advisor gets paid will help you understand his conflicts of interest. All of these arrangements have their pluses and minuses.

I recommend you split up the two functions that are often put together by financial advisors—financial planning and asset management—even if you get them from the same person. Pay for financial planning either with an hourly fee, a flat annual fee, or a single flat fee for putting together a plan. Try to pay for asset management as a flat annual fee, although an AUM fee is acceptable as long as it isn't too high. Just multiply the AUM fee by your assets to determine the total fee. Good asset management is available for as little as $1,000–$5,000 per year. I see little reason to pay $30,000 (1% per year of a $3 million portfolio) a year for it. Expect to pay $200–$400 an hour for financial planning, much of which should be spent face-to-face. If an advisor is charging you $2,000 for a plan or $2,000 a year for financial planning services, he should be spending several hours with you. Fee-only advisory services may be more expensive than buying commissioned products, but at least you're getting good advice for your money. Bad advice is too expensive at any price.

Also beware of the concept that a free lunch is never free. If a potential advisor is offering you a meal or box seats at the game or opera, remember where the money to pay for those things is coming from—clients who have already fallen for his marketing hype! Good investments and good advice are bought, not sold.

## The Value of an Advisor

Expensive financial advisors, even those who give good advice, like to say that they should be paid based on the value they provide. That's like saying a heart surgeon who gives someone ten more years of life should be paid millions for a surgery. Sure, it's a valuable service, but you don't set the price based on the "value." It should be set by the market at a reasonable amount reflective of the education and training of the professional, the risk undertaken by the professional, the work put in by the professional, and the rarity of the professional's skills. If the price is too high, others will train themselves to work in that profession. If too low, fewer will train in the field, and those who are in it already will look around at other options. As the services become rarer, those who perform them can charge more, providing a balance.

An advisor provides a different value to every client. If the value is greater than the fee, then the relationship will persist. If lower, then the relationship should be ended by the client. Only you can decide how much value an advisor is providing for you. There are several ways a good asset manager can provide significant value to the client:

**Five Ways a Good Advisor Can Add Value**

1. Create a solid investing plan
2. Eliminate asset management chores
3. Protect you from yourself
4. Provide reassurance that a professional is on the case
5. Provide access to institutional investments

## 1. Create a solid investing plan

Many clients have little knowledge and even less interest in financial markets, stocks, bonds, portfolios, or retirement accounts. If you know nothing about this "financial stuff" and are willing to pay a significant fee rather than learn it, then the advisor can provide a lot of value for you.

## 2.  Eliminate asset management chores

There are a lot of little chores involved in managing assets even once the plan is set up. You have to decide where to invest new contributions, move money around between accounts, rebalance the portfolio, arrange for appropriate withdrawals, harvest any available tax losses, track your returns, and write up regular portfolio statements. Not having to think about such matters at least once every month or two can be very valuable for many clients.

## 3.  Protect you from yourself

An experienced advisor provides the greatest value by protecting your portfolio from your own behavioral mistakes. Investors are hardwired to buy high and sell low. If you cannot do this yourself but can do it with your advisor's help just once in a big bear market, then the advisor is likely to earn back for you every dollar you ever paid him. He may also keep you from making less-serious financial mistakes as you move through life.

## 4.  Provide reassurance that a professional is on the case

Some clients simply sleep better knowing that there is someone whose job it is to watch their money. Freedom from worry can be very valuable to many people.

## 5.  Provide access to institutional investments

Some of the best advisors provide an additional service by providing access to investments that an investor otherwise wouldn't be able to invest in, such as hedge funds, private equity funds, venture capital funds, and mutual funds from companies like DFA or AQR. Some of these investments should probably be avoided by most investors whether they use an advisor or not, but access to funds you otherwise cannot invest in can be a value provided by the advisor.

## How to Choose an Advisor

The main difficulty with choosing an investment advisor is that by the time you know enough to choose a good one, you probably know enough to do your financial planning and asset management on your own. Some investors end up with a good advisor simply out of luck. But since the vast majority of "advisors" are commissioned salesmen, it is quite easy to luck into a bad advisor.

Many people suggest you ask your colleagues for referrals to good advisors. Personally, I do not think that is a good method. Most of your colleagues cannot tell a good advisor from a bad one. Here are some guidelines that, if followed, will help stack the odds in your favor. There are good advisors that do not meet all of these criteria, and there are probably a few bad advisors that meet them all, but the more of these criteria that the advisor meets, the better the chances are that you have found a quality advisor.

**Nine Criteria to Look For In Your Financial Advisor(s)**

1.  Offers the services you want
2.  Fee-only
3.  Fairly priced
4.  At least one top-tier designation
5.  Gray hair
6.  Knowledge of his limitations
7.  Does not mix insurance and investing
8.  Physician-specific financial planning
9.  Access to institutional funds

### 1.  Offers the services you want

Most doctors seeking financial advisors want someone to "take care of all this money stuff." But there are many different tasks that may be involved, including financial planning, insurance, investment management, tax planning, tax preparation, estate planning, asset protection, etc. There really aren't any advisors that do it all well. When you decide to hire an advisor, figure out FIRST what services you want from them. Hire the right advisor for the right task. Hiring an insurance agent for asset management is probably a mistake, just as hiring an estate planning attorney to sell you disability insurance is a mistake.

## 2. Fee only

Don't hire a commissioned salesman. It is okay to buy your insurance from an independent insurance agent, but you need to decide what kind of insurance you want prior to going to see the agent, lest he sell you the wrong kind. You need to understand exactly how your advisor is paid, whether it is an hourly rate, an annual retainer, or a fee based on assets under management. You may pay for each service in a different manner, such as an hourly rate for financial planning and an annual retainer for asset management or an annual retainer for financial planning and an AUM fee for asset management.

## 3. Fairly priced

Typical hourly rates are in the $200–$400 range. Just like with a physician, that money isn't all take-home due to overhead. Annual retainers start at about $1,000, but anything under $5,000 is still a great price. AUM fees are easily converted to the equivalent of an annual retainer by multiplying the percentage by your assets. For example, a 0.6% fee multiplied by a $750,000 portfolio is $4,500. I think that's a fair price. But 1% multiplied by $2 million is $20,000, which I think is too expensive. It simply isn't a more difficult task to manage that extra $1.25 million. It's the same level of work. The "industry standard" for AUM fees is 1%, but I view that as a maximum, and the percentage should rapidly decrease as AUM grow. If an advisor had just twenty clients with $3 million portfolios and was charging them 1% a year, even with 40% overhead he's still making more than most physicians ($360,000). It simply doesn't take 40 hours x 48 weeks per year /20 clients = 96 hours per client per year to manage assets. Since a computer can do much of it, it probably takes less than a tenth of that to properly service a client. People generally go into the financial services industry because they want to make a lot of money, and many of them do. Their motivations are different from people who go into social work, nursing, and teaching. They will charge you as much as the market will bear. You are the market, so you get to decide what you will bear. It is the advisor's job to make sure you are getting good advice. It is up to you to decide if he is doing it at a fair price.

## 4.  At least one top-tier designation

Financial advisor credentials are a sea of alphabet soup. There are really only three designations used by financial advisors that deserve any significant respect. A Chartered Financial Analyst (CFA) is probably the best designation for an asset manager and the hardest one to get. It isn't much compared with an MD, only requiring about a year of coursework and some work experience, but does require passage of three difficult examinations.

A Certified Financial Planner (CFP©) requires several months of coursework and passage of examinations and is probably the best designation for a financial planner. An insurance-based designation, the Chartered Financial Consultant (ChFC), is similar. It involves slightly more coursework but a less rigorous exam. Other top designations/degrees include a Chartered Life Underwriter (CLU) for an insurance agent, a Juris Doctorate (JD) for an estate planning or asset protection attorney, a Certified Public Accountant (CPA) for tax preparation and advice, and a Master's in Business Administration (MBA), which at least provides management, financial, and accounting education.

I've seen financial advisors with dozens of letters after their names. Most of these are obtained through a weekend seminar or other short course and mean little. Since a top financial designation requires so little effort to obtain, I see little reason for an advisor who really sees doing financial planning or asset management as his career not to obtain at least one of them. In my view, it represents a commitment to the profession.

## 5.  Gray hair

When you are seeking financial advice, you want to be sure to get someone who has adequate experience. You know how steep the learning curve is the first year out of residency. Imagine how steep it is for a 24-year-old financial planner a year out of college. Hire an advisor with at least ten years of experience in giving advice and/or managing assets. That will hopefully ensure he has at least experienced a bear market or two as an advisor (and an investor) and has at least advised clients through most of the common financial dilemmas. If you want someone to teach you successful investing, it helps if they've done it themselves.

## 6.   Knowledge of his limitations

Nobody wants a family doctor who sends all of his diabetics to an endocrinologist and all of his hypertensives to a cardiologist, but you also don't want one who tries to manage a rare neurological disorder on his own. You want a financial planner who can take care of almost everything on his own but is smart enough to know when he needs an accountant or attorney to deal with an issue. The most important limitation of all advisors is that they cannot predict the future. If your advisor seems to be trying to give you the impression that he can, move along to the next one. This means a commitment to a relatively fixed asset allocation composed of low-cost, passive investments, such as index funds. If your advisor thinks he can pick winning stocks, choose winning actively managed mutual funds, or time the market, steer clear!

## 7.   Does not mix insurance and investments

Investing in cash value life insurance or complex annuities is inappropriate for the vast majority of people, including physicians. If anything more than a small percentage of this advisor's clients own these policies, you probably want a different advisor.

## 8.   Physician-specific financial planning

It can be helpful to have a financial planner who advises a number of other physicians. He should be an expert in dealing with student loan issues, such as the Income Based Repayment and the Public Service Loan Forgiveness programs. He should also understand the higher personal and professional liability issues that doctors face. However, you should be aware that most financial issues that doctors face are in no way unique to doctors, and asset management is really no different at all. Most financial advisors who "specialize" in doctors really specialize in marketing to them.

## 9.   Access to institutional funds

Funds from Dimensional Fund Advisors (DFA) and other companies are available only through one of their authorized advisors. If you're going to hire an advisor anyway, you ought to be able to get access to these excellent funds, which in many respects are slightly better than index funds bought at Vanguard and its competitors. One benefit of choosing a DFA-authorized advisor is that DFA has done some of the vetting for you. They only authorize and train advisors who have a commitment to passive investing and staying the course, two important criteria for investment success.

Interacting with financial professionals can be one of the biggest challenges in living the good life. A trusted advisor can be immensely helpful, but high advisory fees can be a difficult hurdle to overcome. There is plenty of middle ground between hiring professionals to do everything and doing it all on your own, but the more you can learn to do yourself, the less you will pay in fees and the better you will get at hiring the right help when you need it.

**Summary of Chapter 10**

- Many financial tasks are easy and profitable do-it-yourself projects. Many physicians competently manage their own personal finances and investments without the assistance of a financial advisor.
- Most who call themselves financial advisors are commissioned stock brokers, mutual fund salesmen, or insurance agents in disguise.
- If you need or want a financial advisor, be sure to hire a fee-only financial advisor.
- Know exactly how and how much you are paying for financial advice and asset management; $1,000–$5,000 per year is a reasonable price.
- Every dollar paid in fees comes directly out of your returns. Don't be afraid to negotiate or ask for a discount.

**Recommended Additional Reading**

Bernstein, W.J. (2010) *The Four Pillars Of Investing*. New York, NY: The McGraw-Hill Companies, Inc.

http://whitecoatinvestor.com/how-to-fire-your-financial-advisor/

http://whitecoatinvestor.com/investing/what-you-need-to-know-about-financial-advisors-2/

# Chapter Eleven
# The Basics of Asset Protection

*"Unfortunately, no matter how frivolous the lawsuit, you still, of course, have to pay people to defend you on it."* — Kelly Ayotte

Physicians need to gain at least a basic understanding of asset protection. Fear of liability not only drives defensive medicine but also causes physicians to make many financial mistakes in their personal lives. As a general rule, physicians are overly concerned with the possibility of being sued for everything they own. The truth is that it is exceedingly rare for a malpractice judgment, especially after appeals, to exceed the policy limits of a typical malpractice insurance policy. It is not something you should be lying awake at night worrying about.

### Balancing Asset Protection with Other Financial Goals

Many naïve physicians assume there is some strategy or vehicle out there that maximizes investment returns, allows for convenient withdrawals, provides for all your estate planning needs, minimizes your taxes, and protects your assets from any possible creditors. Unscrupulous attorneys and insurance agents love to prey on those holding such beliefs. The truth is that there is no such vehicle. You will often have to choose between higher returns or lower taxes. You may have to choose between more flexible withdrawal options and maximum asset protection. The best asset protection plan for you will likely require significant compromises when considered together with your other financial goals.

## Asset Protection Is State Specific

Tort law, that portion of the law concerned with civil suits such as malpractice and personal liability, is state specific. Therefore, any asset protection plan must take into consideration the unique laws and protections available in your state. For example, in Texas, the homestead law protects your residence no matter how expensive (up to 100 acres) from a liability judgment. It also protects two firearms, 12 head of cattle and 120 fowl. North Dakota, however, only protects $80,000 in home equity, and Alabama only protects up to $10,000. Many, but not all states, will protect 100% of your IRA and 401(k) contributions and life insurance cash value. Your plan needs to be specific to your state. If you move to another state, you need to reconsider your plan. See the references at the end of the chapter for a great resource for looking up state-specific asset protection laws.

## Minimizing Risk

Both at work and at home there are practices that will help you to minimize your risk. Practicing good medicine and communicating well with your patients not only prevents damages from ever occurring but also makes patients less likely to sue. Good follow-up and documentation practices can be very useful at preventing lawsuits in the first place.

You can also take steps at home that lower your risk of getting sued. Taken to the extreme, these measures may take all the fun out of life, but fencing off (or even filling in) the pool, getting rid of the trampoline, clearing your walks of snow quickly, not taking your children's friends out on your boat, not serving alcohol at parties, and avoiding dangerous pets will obviously help lower your risk of being sued. No damages, no need to protect assets. Striking a balance between living an enjoyable life with solid asset protection and blatant paranoia can be difficult at times, but taking reasonable precautions (like installing a pool fence and calling a cab for a buzzed driver) is a worthwhile step.

## Insurance Is the First Line of Defense

Even though the risk of a malpractice judgment exceeding your policy limits is extremely low, most physicians will be sued during their career. Many frivolous suits are dismissed, but a significant percentage is simply settled. Malpractice insurance is expensive for a reason—because it gets used to defend you and to pay settlements. Be sure to buy a policy similar to what other physicians in your specialty and state carry. "Going bare" (going without malpractice insurance), where allowed, can be a risky gamble and should only be done as a last resort in an area with ridiculously expensive malpractice premiums. If you do not expect to stay in the same job for a long period of time, then consider getting an "occurrence" policy rather than a "claims-made" policy, which will require a "tail" to be purchased. Occurrence policies will cover liability claims resulting from an act that occurred while you were covered under the policy. Claims-made policies only cover claims brought during the coverage period, and so if a claim is brought after that period, there will be no coverage unless you purchase a tail. A tail may be two to three times the cost of the annual premium for a claims-made policy, so unless an occurrence policy is far more expensive than a comparable claims-made policy or simply unavailable, occurrence is usually the way to go. However, keep in mind that many claims-made policies provide a free tail upon retirement if that occurs after age fifty.

Personal liability can also be a significant issue when physicians are judged, rightly or wrongly, to have "deep pockets." Many states require you to carry automobile liability limits of as little as $50,000. You know as well as I do that it takes very little time in a hospital to run up a bill larger than $50,000. Increase your automobile and homeowner (or renter) insurance policy liability limits to several hundred thousand dollars. Then buy an "umbrella" policy on top of it. For just a few hundred dollars a year, you can have two or three times as much personal liability insurance coverage as you have malpractice insurance coverage. Personal liability coverage does not cover malpractice claims, but it does cover nearly everything else you can be sued for. This is not a place to skimp on coverage. I recommend you carry a $1 million to $5 million umbrella policy above and beyond your auto and homeowner's policy limits. If you can afford it as a resident, get it then, but have a large umbrella policy in place by the time you graduate, even if you still have a negative net worth. Your most valuable asset is your future paychecks, which can be garnished to pay judgments against you.

## Give It Away

The best way to avoid losing something in a lawsuit is not to own it in the first place. Fraudulent transfer laws require this to be done long before the lawsuit comes along, but if you comply with those laws, this is a bulletproof way to protect your assets. Nobody is going to come after money you gave away to charity or to a family member a decade ago. Likewise, a lawsuit that only names you cannot take anything owned solely by your spouse or child. You can give money to your children and still control it until they get older by using Uniform Gift to Minors or Uniform Transfer to Minors Accounts (UGMA/UTMA). 529 accounts are generally protected from creditors, and since you can fund up to five years in advance, you and your spouse can shield up to $140,000 per child from creditors provided you place it there at least two years prior to a successful judgment.

Some useful asset protection techniques use irrevocable trusts. Once an asset is placed into an irrevocable trust, you no longer own it, so it cannot be taken from you as a result of a judgment. The downside, of course, is that you can no longer use the asset, and its growth will be subject to the higher estate tax brackets. Many professionals also like to have most of their assets, including homes, boats, automobiles, bank accounts, and brokerage accounts, solely in their spouse's name. The risk here is that a divorce is far more common than a liability judgment exceeding the limits of your insurance policy. Good luck convincing the divorce judge to give you half of assets that are only in your spouse's name. Titling your assets in only your spouse's name is also useless against a judgment made against both of you.

## Title Your Home Properly

One of the easiest, and cheapest, asset protection techniques is to title your home properly. For married physicians in many states, this will be "John and Jackie Smith, Husband and Wife, Tenants By The Entirety." This means that both John, and Jackie, each own 100% of the home. So a successful lawsuit that only names John cannot take the home, because Jackie owns 100% of it and vice versa. If you are married and your state allows for "tenants by the entirety," be sure to use it. It is free and easy and has the potential to save you hundreds of thousands of dollars.

## Retirement Accounts

I mentioned earlier that there is no "perfect" asset protection vehicle. Your retirement accounts may be the closest you will come. In most states, 100% of the contributions and earnings of your 401(k) and Roth IRAs are completely protected from your creditors. In some states, 401(k)s and rollover IRAs receive significantly better protection from creditors than contributory IRAs and Roth IRAs, so research your state laws before rolling money out of a 401(k) into an IRA, or mixing a rollover IRA and a contributory IRA. Excellent investment options are available in retirement accounts, and the money grows protected from income taxes. Retirement accounts pass to your beneficiary outside of probate and can be "stretched" by your heirs, providing exceptional estate planning benefits. There are numerous circumstances upon which you can withdraw money penalty free from your retirement accounts prior to age 59½. Your qualified retirement account isn't quite as flexible as a taxable investing account, but when you add in the tax, estate planning, and asset protection benefits, it is easy to see that maxing out your retirement accounts is not only the best way to achieve financial security but also to protect your assets in a lawsuit.

## Insurance and Annuities

Cash value life insurance, such as whole life, and other insurance products, such as annuities, can also provide significant asset protection benefits. This benefit is state specific, of course. Many states protect 100% of the cash value, but some (Delaware, New Jersey) protect none of it. Other states may only protect a few thousand dollars of cash value (West Virginia, South Carolina) or require specific beneficiaries (such as the spouse) in order for the assets to be protected. This is an important point to be aware of, since this is one of the main selling points insurance agents use when pushing these products on physicians.

There are two significant downsides to using insurance products for asset protection. Returns tend to be low compared with standard investments inside typical retirement accounts due to the costs of insurance and high fees. In addition, your state insurance guaranty association likely only guarantees a few hundred thousand dollars worth of cash value in the event that the insurance company goes bankrupt. At a certain point, the risk of insurance company bankruptcy outweighs the risk of being sued for more than your insurance limits. One way to help hedge this risk is to own many small policies from different companies just as you should limit your money in any given bank to the amount insured by the FDIC. The additional costs and complexity may not be worth it to you.

## Homestead Laws

As mentioned earlier, different amounts of home equity are protected from creditors by different states. This ranges from essentially all of it (Florida, Texas, Arkansas, Washington, D.C., Iowa, Kansas, Oklahoma, and South Dakota) to almost none of it (Maryland, New Jersey, Pennsylvania) and everything in between. Know the law in your state so that you can make decisions appropriately. For example, a physician with some extra cash in Arkansas may decide to pay down his mortgage (home equity is 100% protected) rather than put that money into his IRA (only $20,000 total is protected from creditors). In North Carolina, the opposite decision would be correct. If home equity is not protected in your state, you may wish to carry a mortgage longer than you otherwise would. An advanced asset protection technique called equity stripping involves taking equity out of your home by refinancing or taking out a home equity loan and placing the proceeds into a retirement account, annuity, or insurance policy. Only you can decide if the additional asset protection is worth the additional expenses and risks.

## Separate Dangerous Assets Using LLCs

Limited liability companies (LLCs) can be used to separate dangerous assets from safe ones. A dangerous asset is one that by its very nature carries substantial liability. Dangerous assets include rental property, recreational vehicles, a side business, and a piece of construction equipment. Safe assets, such as a bank account or home equity, can be seized due to liability caused by a dangerous asset. In order to protect safe assets from dangerous assets, you can place the dangerous asset into an LLC. There generally needs to be a legitimate business reason for the LLC, but for many dangerous assets, such as rental property, there is an obvious business reason. A business owner can even place the real estate for his business into one LLC and the equipment for the business into another LLC. This approach not only protects personal assets from liability incurred by the business assets but also protects one business asset from liability incurred by the other. LLCs are governed by state law, and are easy and relatively inexpensive to set up, even if you use an attorney to assist you.

## Remember Your Biggest Risk

The biggest risk to a physician's assets is divorce. Not only are your current assets at risk but so are your future earnings. A well-known mantra to financial success is "One House, One Spouse." Serial divorces are personally and financially devastating. Put at least as much effort into your marriage as into your practice. Consider a prenuptial agreement to protect yourself, especially if you are marrying after you have acquired significant income or assets or if either of you has children from a prior relationship. Just like an employment contract, nobody needs it when everything works out great.

## Advanced Asset Protection Plans

Most physicians will never need to know more about asset protection than is outlined above. You do not need an attorney for the basics, but definitely get legal advice if you have already been named in a suit, have a high net worth, or if your spouse is also in a high-risk profession, such as medicine. Many doctors need nothing more than a simple asset protection plan.

### A Simple Asset Protection Plan

1. Purchase large quantities of liability insurance
2. Title your home properly
3. Maximize retirement account contributions
4. Pay down mortgage in states with strong homestead laws
5. Avoid owning dangerous assets or minimize liability from them
6. Consider a prenuptial agreement and stay married

However, there are many attorneys and insurance agents out there who would love to sell you more complicated asset protection schemes. These may involve family limited partnerships, offshore trusts, or cash value insurance. If you decide to look into these, be sure to weigh the additional costs and complexity against the asset protection provided and the relatively low risk of actually needing it. Keep in mind that the more complicated and nontraditional your asset protection plan, the more likely future legal changes will require you to pay to have it redone.

Good asset protection plans are, in the words of Douglas Segan, MD, JD, "low risk, simple, traditional, and inexpensive." They are also state specific. Be sure to insure well against liability and learn the applicable laws in your state so that when the inevitable lawsuit crops up, you'll have one less thing to lie awake at night worrying about.

### Summary of Chapter 11

- There is no perfect asset protection plan.
- Increased asset protection often comes at the cost of lower investment returns, more complicated estate planning, or increased taxes.
- Asset protection is state specific. Know your state laws.
- Professional and personal liability insurance is your best defense.
- Maximizing retirement accounts may be the best asset protection plan.
- Marry the right person the first time.

### Recommended Additional Reading

Martin T., Larson P., Larson J. (2012) *Doctor's Eyes Only.* Brockport and Schoolcraft LLC. Chapter 8: Asset Protection Planning.

http://www.assetprotectionbook.com/forum/viewtopic.php?f=142&t=1566

http://www.nolo.com/legal-encyclopedia

http://www.acepnow.com/article/asset-protection-em-physician-consider-10-steps-sued/

# Chapter Twelve
# Estate Planning Made Simple

*"If you don't travel first class, your heirs will!"* — Geoffrey Kent

Estate planning is done for three purposes. The first is to minimize estate taxes. The second, and perhaps the most important, is to ensure that what you want to happen with your children and your assets actually occurs after you die. The final purpose is to avoid the expensive and inconvenient process of probate. Just like asset protection and tax law, estate law frequently changes. Keeping anything but the most basic estate plan up to date will require working with an attorney in your state specializing in this area.

### The Federal Estate Tax

Many doctors fall prey to expensive estate planning solutions provided by unscrupulous insurance agents to help them avoid estate taxes that they won't have to pay anyway. In 2014, the federal estate tax exemption is $5,340,000 ($10,680,000 married). Under current law, this number has been indexed to inflation. So all you have to do to avoid paying federal estate tax is avoid dying with a net worth higher than $5.34M ($10.68M married). Most physicians will never face this problem. They simply don't earn, save, and invest well enough to run into this problem. Even if your net worth starts getting close, it is relatively easy to give money away to your heirs or charity prior to death to stay under the limit.

The gift tax is related to the estate tax, but it isn't a tax you actually pay. It is simply a subtraction from your lifetime estate tax exemption. So if you gave your child a $2 million gift at age eighty and then died with $5.34 million in the bank at age eighty-five, you'd owe estate taxes on that $2 million. But if you died with less than $3.34 million, no tax would be owed. However, you and your spouse are allowed to give away up to $14,000 per year each to as many people as you wish without losing any of your estate/gift tax exemption. If you had four married children and each of them had four married children, you and your spouse could give away up to $1.12 million ($28,000 multiplied by forty people) each year to your family without using up any of your estate tax exemption. There is a special exception for gifts that go into 529 accounts (college savings plans.) You can make five years' worth of contributions ($70,000 per spouse, per beneficiary) in a single year, but you then cannot make a gift to that person for the next five years.

If you are lucky enough, or stupid enough, to die without giving away all your money above the estate tax limits, then the federal government takes 40% of the amount above the exemption. Unless laws change significantly, most physicians won't need much of an estate plan to avoid federal estate taxes.

### State Estate and Inheritance Taxes

Unfortunately, there are nineteen states with estate and/or inheritance taxes, and most of them use lower estate tax exemptions than the federal government. Political types won't be surprised to see that most of these are "blue states" and include Washington, Oregon, Nebraska, Minnesota, Iowa, Illinois, Kentucky, Tennessee, Pennsylvania, New York, Maryland, Delaware, New Jersey, Connecticut, Massachusetts, Rhode Island, Vermont, Maine, and Washington D.C. Inheritance tax is assessed to the person inheriting the money, whereas an estate tax is assessed to the estate prior to the money going to heirs. These laws, like federal estate tax laws, are constantly changing, and the general trend is toward raising the exemption amount, lowering the tax rate, and eliminating the tax completely. However, these states can have exemption amounts as low as $0 (for inheritance taxes) and $675,000 (for estate taxes) and tax rates as high as 18% (for inheritance taxes) and 20% (for estate taxes). If you live in one of these states, keep track of your state's laws since you may need an estate plan to avoid state estate taxes even if your net worth is nowhere near the federal exemption amount.

### Avoiding Estate Taxes

There are many ways to avoid paying these taxes, but nearly all of them involve giving money away to your heirs prior to death directly or using irrevocable trusts or giving money away to charity prior to or at your death. One of the more commonly used methods involves an irrevocable life insurance trust. The owner of a large estate places money into an irrevocable trust (essentially giving it away). The money in the trust is used to pay the premiums on a permanent life insurance policy on the estate owner's life, with his heirs as beneficiaries. Life insurance death benefits are income tax free to heirs and, when inside an irrevocable trust, are also estate tax free.

Another commonly used method is a charitable remainder trust. This involves giving money to a charity, taking an income tax deduction in the year of contribution, receiving (and spending) the income from the donation each year until death, and then upon death, the principal is left to the charity and is thus out of the estate and not subject to estate taxes. There are many other advanced techniques worth looking at if you are lucky enough to have a serious estate tax problem, but most physicians will never need them.

### Step-up in Basis at Death

Another poorly understood estate planning concept is the step-up in basis at death for highly appreciated assets. A simple way to think about basis is that it is what you paid for an asset. When you give a highly appreciated asset (think of a property or shares of a mutual fund you bought for $100,000 that is now worth $500,000) to someone else, they get your basis on the asset, or $100,000. However, if you die and they inherit it, the basis is reset at the value of the asset at the time of your death. They can sell it the next day and won't owe any income tax on it. Giving assets away prior to death is a good way to reduce estate tax, but holding on to assets until death is the best way to reduce income tax.

## The Purpose of a Will

The purpose of a will is to ensure that your money and your minor children go where you want them to go when you die. Everyone needs a will, especially if you have any significant assets, or any minor children. Simple wills can be made using state-specific online forms. If you have significant assets or just want the assurance that the process has been completed correctly, plan to spend a few hundred dollars with an estate planning attorney in your state.

Your will needs to specify the guardian for your children until they reach the age of majority. It also needs to specify a trustee who will manage their assets (assuming you left them some) for their benefit until they reach the age of majority. It is easiest if the guardian is both; however, naming a separate person for each position does enable you to put a "checks and balances" system into place. It also allows you to choose someone who is better with money to be the trustee and someone who will be better at instilling your values in your children to be the guardian.

## Probate

A will is used to specify who gets what if you die. You can give the car to Aunt Nancy, the house to Uncle Ted, and the bank account to Cousin Julie. However, before they get all your stuff, the will must pass through an expensive and lengthy process called probate.

Technically, probate is a document, and "receipt of probate" is the first step in the legal process of administering the estate of the deceased. A probate court decides if the will is valid and then "grants probate" to the executor named in the will, who can then use it as a legal document in carrying out the wishes of the deceased. At any point in this process, the will can be contested. This process is also public knowledge, so anyone can see what you owned after you die. It can also be expensive. Attorneys generally charge a flat fee, an hourly rate, or a percentage of the estate, sometimes as high as 8%. Probate will require three months at a minimum but more likely closer to a year. It is not unusual for a probate case, especially if contested, to take one to three years or longer. It is easy to see why it might be wise to avoid having to go through probate, at least with most of your assets. Certainly having a will is better than "dying intestate" (without a will), but ensuring your assets don't have to pass through the probate process is a worthwhile endeavor. There are two ways to do this—naming specific beneficiaries and using a revocable trust.

### Naming Beneficiaries

Insurance policies, retirement plans such as IRAs and 401(k)s, and many brokerage and bank accounts allow you to name a beneficiary. Assets with named beneficiaries go directly to your heirs without passing through the probate process. For many of us, this can be the vast majority of our assets, greatly simplifying the process of settling your estate. Jointly titling assets in the proper manner with heirs can also enable them to pass outside of probate, but it may eliminate the step-up in basis the heir would otherwise get.

### The Purpose of a Revocable Trust

The main benefit of a revocable trust (meaning you can remove your assets from the trust at any time) is that assets placed into a revocable trust do not have to pass through probate. Unlike an irrevocable trust, assets in a revocable trust haven't been given away, so they don't help you reduce estate tax due, and they don't protect assets from creditors. Compared with a will, a revocable trust is more difficult to contest, more private, and more expensive to set up, but administering the trust upon your death is cheaper and much faster than probating a will.

### Healthcare Power Of Attorney

Nearly everything I have read about estate planning talks about making sure you have a living will and a healthcare power of attorney and attorneys often include these in a comprehensive estate plan. As an emergency doctor, I have been involved with many end of life decisions, and I do not recall a single one where a living will or a healthcare power of attorney was of much use. If you are capable of making your own healthcare decisions, I ask you what you want to do. If you are not capable of doing so, I ask the family members, friends, or partner present (people who presumably care about you the most) what they think you would like done in this type of situation. If there is no one present, I do what I think most reasonable people would want done. Unless you have a very unusual situation, I suggest that rather than paying an attorney to draw up some formal documents (or even using an inexpensive online solution) that you simply tell your family what you would want done in the event you are not capable of making your own healthcare decisions. The main issue I run into is not that there is no formal document. It is that the patient and his family never had this conversation before I asked them outside Trauma Room One if Grandpa Smith would want to be intubated if it meant he would probably be on a ventilator the rest of his life. I suspect your experiences are similar.

Estate planning is a little bit like buying life insurance. You should really only have to deal with it a few times in your life. Few physicians will need anything more than a will, a revocable trust, and an understanding of the federal and state estate tax exemption amounts.

## Summary of Chapter 12

- Estate planning is done to minimize estate tax, avoid probate, and ensure your assets and your minor children go where you want them to when you die.
- Most physicians won't owe any federal estate tax even without an estate plan.
- Most estate planning techniques involve giving your assets away while still retaining some control over them.
- Most physicians should probably have a will and a revocable trust.

## Recommended Additional Reading

Sharp, R.F. (2010) *Living Trusts For Everyone: Why a will is not the way to avoid probate, protect heirs, and settle estates.* New York, NY : Allworth Press.

Martin T., Larson P., Larson J. (2012) *Doctor's Eyes Only.* Brockport and Schoolcraft LLC. Chapter 7: Estate Planning

http://whitecoatinvestor.com/introduction-to-estate-planning/

http://www.forbes.com/sites/ashleaebeling/2013/11/01/where-not-to-die-in-2014-the-changing-wealth-tax-landscape/

http://www.nolo.com/legal-encyclopcdia/wills

# Chapter Thirteen
# Income Taxes and the Physician

*Not all tax questions have clear-cut answers....When you have a choice between two legal [tax] alternatives, choose the one which results in the lowest tax."* — John T. Reed

Almost every physician I've ever met thinks he pays too much in taxes. Most of them are right no matter what their political persuasion. The reason isn't just that the tax code is progressive and doctors have a high income. It is also that many physicians do not have even a basic understanding of the tax code. You don't need a CPA to know enough about the tax code to lower your taxes dramatically.

### Four Reasons I Do My Own Taxes

Most physicians pay somebody else to do their own taxes. I think that's fine. I never have a problem with someone paying a fair price for good advice and quality service. However, I do my own taxes for four reasons.

The first, and most important, is that doing my own taxes over the years has helped **me understand how the tax code works.** While not everything about taxes makes sense, once you understand the underlying reasons why one person pays more tax than another, you can make some changes in how you live your financial life that will lower your taxes.

The second reason I do my own taxes is simply that I can think of a better use for the $1,000 or more that I would have to pay a high-quality tax preparer to do my increasingly complicated tax return. For many doctors, **tax preparation fees** may represent the income from an entire day or more of work that you're sacrificing so someone else can fill out some paperwork for you.

The third reason I do my own taxes is that **I enjoy it**. Every year it's a game, the IRS versus me, and as my sisters and childhood friends will tell you, I love competition just for the sake of competition.

The fourth reason is that I have much **more incentive to lower my taxes than a paid tax preparer** does. He is getting a flat fee or perhaps an hourly rate, but every dollar saved in taxes goes straight back into my wallet.

I would encourage you to do your own taxes at least once. Even better, do them on paper without the assistance of tax software. You will be surprised how much you learn about money, the tax code, and how our government works. If you start as a medical student and continue on, you will find that you only need to learn one or two new things a year and before you know it, filling out Schedules A, B, C, D, E, and SE is no more difficult than draining a simple abscess. You can always pay a CPA to check your work and make suggestions. Then if you want to pay someone to eliminate that hassle from your life in future years, at least you know what you are paying them to do. Once you have done it on paper once, tax software can be very useful to pull in the prior year's information, eliminate math errors, and allow you to look at alternative scenarios.

### How to Lower Your Taxes

The average physician has a gross income in the $200,000 range. In 2012, I made more than that yet paid less than 9% of my income in federal income tax. I wrote a blog post about it, and many who read it were amazed that the figure could be so low. They couldn't figure out how I did it. It was easy; I read a book on taxes. It was terribly boring, even for someone interested in personal finance and investing. However, over the course of the decades I spent in school, I learned that it is often worthwhile to read and understand boring material, you know, like Nephrology and Pulmonology. If I handed you a thick book at the beginning of your career and told you that reading it would pay you hundreds of thousands of dollars over your career, would you read it? Of course you would no matter how boring it was. That's what reading a book on taxes will do for you.

I turns out that the federal government wants you to do some very specific things and will reward you for doing them. These specific things are written into the federal tax code. Can you list ten or fifteen of them? If not, you need to read a book on taxes. If you do not do them, you will be punished in the form of paying higher taxes. Let's take a look at some of these things:

**How to Lower Your Tax Bill**

- Get married
- Have children
- Have a stay-at-home parent
- Buy a home with a mortgage
- Pay property and state income taxes
- Save for retirement
- Save for college
- Consume healthcare
- Spread your lifetime income over as many years as possible
- Invest for the long term
- Start a business
- Own rental property
- Give money to charity

I do all of these. In effect, the government subsidizes my life because I've chosen to live my life the way the government wants me to live it. Investors have the maxim "Don't fight the Fed," which basically means to take investment risk when the Fed is encouraging you to do so. Taxpayers should have a similar maxim—"Don't fight the IRS."

## Tax Breaks Are Not All Equal

Doctors are often familiar with tax deductions and credits, but I find they generally have no ability to compare one tax break to another. First, it is important to understand the difference between a tax deduction and a tax credit. A **tax deduction,** such as the student loan interest deduction, the charitable contribution deduction, or the business expense deduction, is money on which you don't pay taxes. If you give $2,000 to a charity, you won't owe income taxes on that $2,000 of income (a $500 savings if your marginal tax rate is 25%). A **tax credit** is money paid toward your tax bill. So a $2,000 tax credit is $2,000 directly subtracted from your tax bill. So credits are better than deductions.

There are also different categories of deductions. Business expense deductions, which generally show up on Schedule C, are subtracted directly from your business income. You don't have to pay payroll (Social Security and Medicare) taxes or income taxes on that money. "Above the line" deductions, such as the self-employed health insurance deduction, show up on the front page of the 1040 and is superior to a "below the line" deduction, such as mortgage interest, which shows up on Schedule A. The "line" is Line 37 on Form 1040, the line at the bottom of the first page. The "standard deduction" replaces all of your below the line deductions. You can either "itemize" your below the line deductions or just take the standard deduction. However, even if you take the standard deduction, you still get to count all your above the line deductions, so above the line deductions are worth more than below the line deductions.

However, even two deductions that are in the same category can be dramatically different in size. For instance, you may have given $300 to a charity, but you paid $21,000 in mortgage interest. One of those may save you $100 in taxes, while the other saves you $7,000.

## The Best Deduction

It makes no sense to pay $1.00 for something in order to save thirty-three cents in tax. You will go broke very quickly using that philosophy. However, if you are going to buy something anyway, then making that purchase tax deductible is the very best deduction out there. For instance, my Internet bill is about $60 a month. I had it before I started The White Coat Investor website. However, once I started the business, the Internet bill became a business expense. At a 33% marginal tax rate, claiming that deduction is $20 a month in my pocket. Free money. (Technically, I can only deduct the portion actually used for business purposes.)

### The Biggest Deduction

The biggest but perhaps most underutilized deduction among physicians is the simple act of maxing out your available tax-deferred accounts. I quantified my tax savings from various factors in 2012. I saved $4,000 in taxes by owning my home instead of renting. Being married saved me about $7,000. Having three children saved me about $3,000 in taxes. Owning a business saved me about $1,000. However, saving for retirement saved me a whopping $20,000 in income taxes. This is the quickest and easiest way for a physician to reduce his income tax bill. If the physician has a marginal tax rate of 33%, putting $6,550 into a H.S.A., $52,000 into a 401(k)/Profit-sharing Plan, and $50,000 into a cash balance/defined benefit plan (another type of tax-deferred retirement plan available to many physicians) will reduce his tax bill by nearly $36,000. That may be more than two months' pay for many physicians. The best part about the deduction for retirement plan contributions is that you still have the money. You didn't even have to spend it to get the deduction.

### Marginal versus Effective Tax Rates

It is very important for the financially astute physician to understand the concept of a marginal tax rate and tax brackets and particularly how that differs from your effective tax rate. Your **marginal tax rate** is the rate at which the last dollar you make is taxed. Your **effective tax rate** is the total amount you pay in taxes divided by your gross income. Consider a married physician with a gross household income of $200,000 who takes the standard deduction. Table 8 shows how his money will be taxed.

His marginal tax rate will be 28%, but his effective tax rate is only 19%. The effective tax rate on the first $100,000 he made was less than 12%, and the effective tax rate on the second $100,000 was 26%, averaging out to 19%.

| Income | Tax Rate | Tax |
|---|---|---|
| First $20,300 | 0% | $0 |
| Next $18,150 | 10% | $1,815 |
| Next $55,650 | 15% | $8,348 |
| Next $75,050 | 25% | $18,763 |
| Last $30,850 | 28% | $8,638 |
| Total $200,000 | 19% | $37,564 |

**Table 8**

The marginal tax rate is important, because it helps you make decisions "at the margin." However, the effective tax rate has much more to do with the actual amount of taxes paid. Many physicians ignorantly fear "getting bumped into the next tax bracket," but as you can see, this makes no sense because only the money in that highest tax bracket is actually taxed at the higher rate. It doesn't cause all of your money to be taxed at your marginal tax rate. Doctors in the 33% tax bracket aren't actually paying 33% of their income in federal income tax.

This example illustrates one of the great advantages of using a tax-deferred retirement account, such as a 401(k). You get to save taxes at your marginal rate and later pay them at a lower effective rate (technically a blend of multiple lower marginal rates), assuming no other taxable income. Your 401(k) withdrawals are used to "fill up" the lower tax brackets. Saving 33% on your contributions and then paying 0%, 10%, 15%, or even 25% on the withdrawals is a winning formula.

### Aggressive Tax Reduction

Many physicians are inappropriately terrified of a tax audit. Don't get me wrong. An audit can be time consuming, unpleasant, and even expensive. However, if you take the proper perspective, you'll realize that paying taxes is really an annual negotiation with the government. You get the opportunity to make the first offer. That's what you put at the bottom of your 1040. Twenty-four times out of twenty-five, the government takes this offer. And 4% of the time, they make a counter offer. That's called an audit. You can simply take the counter offer, pay the additional tax they say you owe (plus any applicable penalties and interest), and move on with life. You can negotiate back and forth with the auditor a few times. Then, you can either accept the outcome of the negotiation or you can go to tax court. The auditor cannot force you to pay the taxes, and he cannot throw you in jail. His only power is to make you go over his head to tax court. There, you get the chance to make your case again. If the judge rules against you, then you have to pay the tax within a few months. In the meantime, you had the use of that extra money for about two years. On average, the taxpayer pays 27% of what the IRS sought in tax court. Don't be afraid to fight, assuming you have a legitimate case. Don't consider it a legal decision; consider it a business decision. It isn't about proving your innocence; it's about money.

Just like any other negotiation, it pays real money to be aggressive. There are many "gray areas" in the tax code. It is important that you learn the subject well enough to recognize what is gray and what is black and white but you're simply ignorant of. Then, if you're looking at something in the gray area, call it in your favor. Since they just take your first offer most of the time, you're better off being aggressive. Now, I'm not advocating cheating on your taxes. Tax evasion is a crime, and you can go to jail for it. The IRS, however, does not throw people in jail for simple errors or for arguing about a truly gray area. If the law says you have to pay, then pay. As John T. Reed, author of *Aggressive Tax Avoidance for Real Estate Investors,* likes to say, "I'll pay every cent I owe, but I'm not going to leave a tip." If fact, Mr. Reed states he would love to see the IRS do a lot more audits since he doesn't cheat on his taxes despite the fact that lots of people do. It is estimated that auditors generate far more income for our government than they cost. If auditors could get everyone to pay the tax they owe, all of our taxes could be lower.

However, if the law isn't clear about whether taxes are owed or not, then call it in your favor. Your tax preparer may not want to do this. If you don't tell him otherwise, he may assume you'd rather pay more in taxes than increase the possibility of an audit even a tiny bit. He certainly doesn't want to spend his time and money defending you in an audit, especially if he "guarantees" his return by offering that service for free. So his incentive is to be less aggressive than he probably ought to be with the gray areas.

Some tax deductions, such as a home office, business mileage, and large charitable donations, are widely thought to be "audit triggers" because they are frequently abused. However, if you legitimately qualify for these deductions and have the documentation to prove it, it seems foolish to me not to take them. If the deductions were only going to save you fifty dollars in taxes, it would be one thing not to claim them in order to slightly decrease the chance of an audit. But if it were a matter of saving $5000 per year in taxes, I would rather go through one audit every couple of decades than pay an extra $100,000 in taxes. Critics complain that this will cause the IRS to look at the rest of your tax return at the same time. This is generally not the case, since auditors usually only look at two or three items per return, but even if it were, why is that a big deal if you have been legitimately trying to pay every cent you legally owe in taxes?

### Payroll Taxes

Payroll taxes include Social Security tax (6.2% from the employee and 6.2% from the employer on the first $117,000 of earned income) and Medicare tax (1.45% from the employee and 1.45% from the employer on all of your income). If you are self-employed, you pay both halves, but the employer half is deductible. Two earners, even if they file their taxes as "Married Filing Jointly," still have to pay Social Security tax on each of their first $117,000 of earnings. Payroll taxes are due on all earned income, including money put into retirement plans. You do not, however, owe payroll taxes on unearned income, such as rent from an income property or dividends.

The fact that Social Security tax isn't owed on a large percentage of a physician's income flattens our progressive tax brackets considerably. For example, consider a single independent contractor physician without dependents taking the standard deduction. His marginal tax rate, including payroll taxes but not state income taxes, will be about 41% as he approaches the $117,000 limit. However, just after that limit, his marginal tax rate drops to 30% and doesn't reach 41% again until his taxable income is over $400,000! The bottom line is that marginal tax rates are quite flat for a self-employed single person beginning at about $40,000 and are in fact lowest in the $117,000–$200,000 range. With careful tax planning, a large percentage of physicians can arrange for their taxable income to be within this range.

Decreasing the amount of tax you pay unnecessarily may be an easy way to get more money in your pocket. Understanding the basics of the tax code is important even if you choose to pay someone else to do your taxes.

**Summary of Chapter 13**

* A basic understanding of the tax code can pay big dividends.
* Don't spend money you otherwise would not just to get a tax deduction.
* By learning what is deductible, you can pay for many of your expenses with pretax dollars.
* Maximizing your retirement plan contributions provides a large tax reduction.
* It is critical to understand the difference between your marginal tax rate and your effective tax rate.
* Be aggressive when trying to reduce your tax bill.

**Recommended Additional Reading**

Reed, J.T. (2009) *Aggressive Tax Avoidance for Real Estate Investors.* Alamo, CA: John T. Reed.

Piper, M. (2013) *Taxes Made Simple: Income Taxes Explained in 100 Pages or Less.* St. Louis, MO: Simple Subjects LLC.

Lasser, J.K. (2013) *Your Income Tax 2014.* Hoboken, NJ: John Wiley & Sons, Inc.

http://whitecoatinvestor.com/10-reasons-why-i-pay-less-tax-than-mitt-romney/

*http://whitecoatinvestor.com/taxes/tax-diversification-2/*

*http://whitecoatinvestor.com/7-tax-deductions-doctors-miss-out-on/*

# Chapter Fourteen
# Choosing a Business Structure

*"Being good in business is the most fascinating kind of art. Making money is art and working is art and good business is the best art."*
— Andy Warhol

More and more physicians are becoming employees of hospitals and other large organizations. From 1996 to 2005, the proportion of physicians with an ownership stake in their practice declined from 62% to 55% according to a study by the Center for Studying Health Center Change. That trend has only accelerated over the last decade, and in many communities, more than 90% of the physicians are employees. Physicians who have never been anything other than an employee of a large organization and don't plan to ever be a business owner can skip the rest of this chapter.

Now that those guys are gone, I'll let you in a on a little secret. As a general rule, business owners make more than employees, at least as long as the business is profitable. The reason why is clear. Why would you hire an employee if it cost you more to hire him than he brought into the business as profit? Profit is the difference between what you pay your employees and the income they produce. If employees are paid exactly what they produce, there won't be any profit for the business owner.

## Why Hospitals Are Employing Physicians

There is a current practice in medicine, however, that bucks this trend. Hospitals are hiring physicians and paying them more than they are generating in physician fees and often more than they would make in their own practice. The hospital can do this because it then controls the physician and where he refers his patients, what tests he orders, what treatments he prescribes, when he takes call, and how he chooses to hospitalize his patients. Along with this control, the hospital can now tack on "facility fees" to what used to be outpatient clinic visits. Due to this current practice, more physicians are becoming hospital employees each year. While bad for physician independence and cost control, it has been a positive for physician incomes thus far. However, the long-term effect of fewer and fewer physicians owning their own businesses is not encouraging.

## The Physician Business Owner

There are still plenty of physicians out there who work as independent contractors, partners, and practice owners. These doctors often struggle with understanding the difference between independent contractor, sole proprietor, partnership, limited liability company (LLC), S Corporation, and C Corporation. This chapter will help you understand the difference between all of these business structures and help you decide which one is right for you.

## No Malpractice Protection

One common misunderstanding among physicians is that choosing the right structure will somehow protect them from malpractice lawsuits. Unfortunately, that is not the case. All malpractice is personal. No corporate structure will protect you from it. You must insure against this risk, self-insure it, or plan to declare bankruptcy if you're ever sued. Incorporating won't help.

## Employee versus Independent Contractor

There are two broad categories for employment. You can be an employee where you are paid on IRS Form W-2, much like when you were a resident. Alternatively, you can be self-employed as an independent contractor, where you are generally paid on Form 1099.

As an employee, your employer usually pays for some benefits, such as health insurance, dental insurance, and even retirement plan matching contributions. The employer also pays half of your payroll taxes (6.2% of the first $117,000 toward Social Security and 1.45% of all earnings toward Medicare).

As an independent contractor, you must purchase your own benefits and pay both halves of payroll taxes. You do get to deduct these costs on your taxes, but you should still expect to be paid significantly more as an independent contractor than as an employee. One of the best parts of being an independent contractor is that you control what benefits you purchase. It isn't hard to select a better retirement plan than your employer will offer you, and you don't have to pay for benefits you may not value, such as group disability and life insurance.

On a typical physician income of $200,000, I would expect to be paid about 10% more as an independent contractor than an employee to make up for these additional costs. The higher your salary, the lower this percentage can be for it to be a square deal since the cost of benefits and Social Security taxes are fixed.

## Non-malpractice Liability Protection

The most basic business entity is the sole proprietor. If you are hired as an independent contractor and you do not set up anything else, this is what you are. You are legally liable for any liability your business incurs. If you don't have any employees, this liability is fairly low, but it isn't zero. Sole proprietorship is a perfectly reasonable business structure for a single physician without employees.

If you go into business with somebody else as a legal entity known as a partnership, you are not only responsible for your own mistakes but also those of your partner(s). For this reason, any business with employees or with more than one owner is best structured as an LLC or corporation. That way, if the business is sued, nothing more than the business can be lost. LLCs are regulated by the individual states, but in general setting up an LLC is more simple than incorporating and provides the same legal protections for the owners, while providing a simpler way to pay taxes. Many states require physicians, attorneys, and similar professionals to have a Professional Limited Liability Company (PLLC), but there is no significant difference.

## Tax Savings Available With Various Business Structures

There are really three models of taxation available with various business structures: sole proprietor, S Corporation, or C Corporation.

As a **sole proprietor or partner,** all of the income from the business is passed through to you each year, and you are responsible for the taxes on that income, paid at your regular income tax rates. Payroll taxes are due on all of your income.

If you incorporate, you may elect to be taxed as an **S Corporation.** An S Corp is also a pass-through entity, so all income goes to the corporation owner each year. The difference between an S Corp and a sole proprietorship is that an S Corp owner may elect to have some of his income paid to him as a salary and some of it paid as a "dividend." You do not have to pay payroll taxes on the dividends. For example, if your S Corporation earns $250,000 in profit, you may choose to pay yourself $150,000 in salary and $100,000 in dividends. By doing so, you will not have to pay Medicare taxes on $100,000, saving yourself $2,900 in taxes. In order to minimize taxes, you want to get paid as little salary as possible and as much dividend as possible. Of course, the IRS is not stupid. They expect you to pay yourself a reasonable salary, although audits on this subject aren't particularly common. How low can you go? The IRS has no guidelines on the subject. They simply say that your salary must be reasonable and appropriate. The various courts that have ruled on this question have considered various factors in making a determination.

**Factors Considered When Determining a Reasonable Salary**

- Training and experience
- Duties and responsibilities
- Time and effort devoted to the business
- Dividend history
- Payments to non-shareholader employees
- Timing and manner of paying bonuses to key people
- What comparable businesses pay for similar services
- Compensation agreements
- The use of a formula to determine compensation

Here are six common sense recommendations for determining your salary.

1. Don't pay yourself less than **half of your income** as salary.

2. Don't pay yourself less than the **Social Security maximum** taxable income as salary ($117,000 for 2014). You will have a hard time convincing a court that a physician salary should be less than this. Plus, you will decrease your eventual Social Security payments.

3. The more of your income that comes from the **work of others,** the lower your salary to income ratio can be. For example, if you employ P.A.'s or other physicians, sell products out of your clinic, or provide ancillary services, such as lab or X-ray, then it is easier to justify a lower ratio.

4. S Corp dividends cannot be used for income calculations that determine **how much income you can put into a retirement plan,** such as a 401(k)/Profit-sharing plan. If you pay yourself too little, you will save on Medicare tax but lose the tax, asset protection, and estate planning benefits of maxing out your retirement plan. Maxing out a Solo 401(k) in 2013 with a contribution of $51,000 required an income of about $177,000. A SEP IRA required a higher income, about $266,000 in 2013 in order to contribute the maximum $51,000. As the contribution limit rises with inflation, the income requirement will also increase.

5. **Have a formula** for compensation and written documentation of how you determined your salary. Obtain a copy of a **salary survey** for your

specialty. You can then use the average hourly rate or average salary for a physician in your specialty as the basis for your determination.

6.    If your salary to income ratio is too high, the tax savings may not justify the additional hassle and cost of incorporation. If you cannot **justify at least $100,000 in dividends,** then I would not bother incorporating for tax savings.

**C Corporations** also provide a unique method of taxation. A C Corp is not a pass-through entity. It may retain its earnings inside the corporation instead of paying them out to the owner each year as a salary. However, a C Corp is subject to its own, more progressive, tax bracket system. Corporate tax rates are as low as 15% for the first $50,000 and only 25% up to $75,000. However, if the primary business your corporation is involved in is medical care, the IRS calls you a "personal service corporation," and everything the corporation earns (and doesn't pay you as salary) is taxed at 35%. In addition, when the corporation distributes dividends to you, you may pay as much as 23.8% on the dividends, for a total tax rate of 50.5%! Does that sound like a way to save on taxes? For this reason, a C Corp is a poor choice of business entity for a physician.

An **LLC or PLLC** may choose to be taxed as a sole proprietor, an S Corp, or a C Corp. In addition, essentially all the same business expense deductions are available to you as a sole proprietor, partner, LLC, S Corp, or C Corp. You do not have to incorporate to deduct your CME costs and other legitimate business expenses.

### Which Should You Choose?

If you are an independent contractor physician, I suggest you choose sole proprietorship, or if you think the Medicare tax savings will justify the hassle, as S Corp or LLC choosing to be taxed as an S Corp. If you are in a partnership or have employees, an LLC or corporation structure is important for the liability protection.

Choosing the proper business entity can protect you from some business-related (but not malpractice) liability and save you a few bucks on taxes. However, the benefits of incorporation are not nearly as large as most physicians think.

## Summary of Chapter 14

- Your business structure will not provide any malpractice protection.
- An S corporation can pay dividends instead of salary, saving payroll taxes.
- A sole proprietorship is fine for most physician independent contractors.
- Most physician groups will likely want an LLC or corporate structure in place.
- C corporations do not make much sense for physicians.

### Recommended Additional Reading

Piper, M. (2013) *Independent Contractor, Sole Proprietor, and LLC Taxes Explained in 100 pages or Less*. St. Louis, MO: Simple Subjects LLC.

http://whitecoatinvestor.com/downsides-of-a-c-corporation/

# Chapter Fifteen
# Enjoying the Good Life

*"To laugh often and love much; to win the respect of intelligent persons and the affection of children; to earn the approbation of honest citizens and endure the betrayal of false friends; to appreciate beauty; to find the best in others; to give of one's self; to leave the world a bit better, whether by a healthy child, a garden patch or a redeemed social condition; to have played and laughed with enthusiasm and sung with exultation; to know even one life has breathed easier because you have lived—this is to have succeeded."* — Bessie Anderson Stanley

If you've followed the suggestions given to you thus far in this book, it won't be long before you find yourself five or ten years out of residency in an enviable financial position. Not only will you have a high income, but you will also have a seven-figure net worth, and your only debt will be an affordable mortgage. At a certain point, you'll need to decide what you want out of life. Your long planned for financial stability will provide you many opportunities to choose from.

## Freedom from Financial Worry

While you will not be able to retire just a few years out of residency, hopefully that was not your goal upon entering the lengthy pipeline you had to pass through in order to practice your profession. You do not have enough money to do nothing, but you do have enough to do anything reasonable that you wish to do.

You do not have to live like a resident forever; eventually, you can grow into most of your income. This means you can buy some of those niceties that you have deferred for so long. You can save adequately for retirement and still spend a ton of money eating out, going on vacation, giving to charity, or buying fancy cars, expensive toys, or custom-made furniture. You cannot have it all at once, but one thing at a time you can enjoy the good life. Carve that 20% off the top, and spend the rest in accordance with your values without a bit of guilt.

## Your Dream Job

One of the best things about having little debt and plenty of assets is that you can take your dream job. That might be a job in a location that doesn't pay well. It might be a job in academics, where you can spend time researching or teaching rather than cranking patients through a clinic. It might be sharing a job, working part-time, or spending a few years on the "mommy track." It might just be the freedom to tell an onerous hospital administrator to "shove it" when he tries to interfere with the appropriate practice of medicine. It may also be the opportunity to work a day a week in a volunteer clinic, keep seeing patients you like who can't afford to pay you, or go on medical mission trips.

## Transitioning Out Of Medicine

Many physicians find that after a decade or two of practice, they really are not enjoying medicine much. Based on some of the griping I hear on online physician forums, that might be the MAJORITY of doctors! Getting yourself on the right financial track very early in your career will provide you the freedom you will almost surely want later. This might be the ability to go part-time or cut back on call. It might allow you to transition to a nonmedical career you will enjoy more despite a lower salary. There is also the possibility of early retirement. While very few doctors will ever be able to retire completely at forty, retiring at fifty is a very doable goal for a physician who went to medical school in his twenties. Being in control of your financial life means you can control your own destiny, and isn't that what we all want?

**Summary of Chapter 15**

- Managing your finances well early in your career will prevent financial worries and provide many open doors in the last half of your career.

**Recommended Additional Reading**

http://whitecoatinvestor.com/protecting-the-ability-of-physicians-to-practice-medicine/

# Chapter Sixteen
# The Mission of
# The White Coat Investor

*"Knowledge is power. Information is liberating. Education is the premise of progress, in every society, in every family."* — Kofi Annan

I started The White Coat Investor blog in the spring of 2011 to help physicians get a "fair shake" on Wall Street. The average doctor is at a marked disadvantage in his interactions with stock brokers, lenders, insurance agents, realtors, investment advisors, and similar financial professionals for three reasons.

First, physicians have little to no training in business, finance, and investing, so the information asymmetry between the two parties in the transaction is often extreme.

Second, physicians are busy, and most would honestly prefer not to deal with these subjects at all. They do not mind paying a fair price for someone to take this hassle away from them. Unfortunately, that is difficult to do because it requires a certain amount of education and hassle to understand the difference between good advice and bad, and even good advice is frequently offered at too high of a price.

Finally, physicians are entirely too trusting of other professionals. We are used to trusting our consultants in areas that we know little about. The difference in ethical standards between the gastroenterologist you are consulting with and the typical insurance agent is unfortunately rather profound.

As a general rule, people do not go into the financial fields for the same reasons that other people become kindergarten teachers, nurses, or even physicians. There is no equivalent to the medical school application essay, where they explain why they want to help people. As Bill Bernstein has famously explained, "If you assume that every financial professional you interact with is a hardened criminal, you'll do okay." That's not to say there are not talented and ethical advisors, insurance agents, mortgage lenders, and realtors out there. There are plenty of them, even if they are a minority of their profession. It is an unfortunate truth that the vast majority of financial professionals receive most of their training in sales and marketing rather than finance or investing.

It is becoming more and more difficult to be the kind of physician we all ought to be and still be able to live "the good life." It costs more to get into the business, it pays less once you're in it, and the regulatory hassles and liability at times seem to be exponentially increasing. I believe that a good portion of these downsides for physicians can be offset with better personal financial planning and investing knowledge and habits. If my generation of doctors can finally shed their reputation as poor money managers and investors, I'll consider The White Coat Investor a success.

You can help advance the mission of The White Coat Investor primarily by spreading the word. Help our students and residents get the information they need early in their career when they most need it. While I don't expect business, finance, or investing education to be added to the medical school curriculum anytime soon, there are plenty of opportunities for mentors to pass along a few pearls, give a useful book, or recommend a website. It's okay to tell colleagues that you are a do-it-yourself investor, and they can learn to do many of their financial chores without professional assistance. When the student is ready, the teacher will appear.

You can also help ethical, knowledgeable financial professionals be more successful by recommending them to colleagues. There are some good people in these industries who are trying to clean it up. They charge a fair price for good advice and service. Let's help them run everyone else out of business.

The good life is out there—a wonderful career, financial freedom, a few simple luxuries, and a retirement free of financial worry. However, it isn't a default setting for a physician. You have already done 90% of the work to get it. That last 10% is simply managing your finances and investments well. Commit now to do so.

**Summary of Chapter 16**

- Physicians have several challenges to overcome when interacting with financial professionals.
- Physicians are often considered "whales," "marks," or "suckers" by financial "professionals."
- Learning about finance and investing will improve your personal life and career.
- Share your financial knowledge with trainees and other physicians.
- Pass this book along to one of your colleagues.

# Questions or Comments?

I would love to hear your thoughts on this book. Errors will be corrected and suggestions incorporated into future editions. Email me at editor@whitecoatinvester.com.

## Need help?

If you need assistance finding a financial professional who gives good advice at a fair price, contact me at the above email address or come by http//whitecoatinvestor.com.

While it is impossible to run a for-profit website without any financial conflicts of interest, you will find that every one of mine is fully disclosed on the site, including an annual statement displaying the source of every dollar I made that year.

## Sign Up For the Blog Feed and Newsletter

The White Coat Investor blog regularly posts as many as three posts per week written by yours truly as well as by many experts in insurance, investing, asset protection, estate planning, and personal finance. All of the content is completely free to you, and by subscribing you can have it show up effortlessly in your email box or RSS feed. You can sign up at http://feeds.feedburner.com/The White CoatInvester.

I also write a free monthly email newsletter that includes a market report, links to the best financial stuff on the Internet for doctors, and tips and advice not found on the regular blog. You can sign up for that at http://whitecoatinvestor.com/free-monthly-newsletter/.

## One Last Thing . . .

If you feel particularly strongly about the contributions this book has made to your own financial knowledge, I'd be grateful if you posted a review on Amazon.

Sincerely,

Jim

Made in the USA
Middletown, DE
27 October 2017